Martha's Vineyard Miracles

Martha's Vineyard Miracles

A True Story of Magic & Madness

Paul Samuel Dolman

South Beach

SOUTH BEACH PUBLISHING

Published by South Beach (USA)

404 Sweet Magnolia Court

Saint Augustine, Florida 32080

First printing, July 2015

Copyright © 2015 by Paul Samuel Dolman

LIBRARY OF CONGRESS CATALOGING-IN-PUBLICATION DATA

ISBN 978-1-890115-02-9

Printed in the United States of America
Cover Design and Interior Layout by Matthew Wayne Selznick

While the author has made every effort to provide accurate telephone numbers, Internet addresses, and other contact information at the time of publication, neither the publisher nor the author assumes any responsibility for errors or for changes that occur after publication. Further, the publisher does not have any control over and does not assume any responsibility for author or third-party websites or their content

FOR...

THE SUCHS...

KATHERINE, MY SPIRIT SISTER...

AND ALL THOSE WHO SEEK TO LOVE
WITH AN OPEN HEART AND KIND SOUL

I STILL BELIEVE IN MIRACLES

Martha's Vineyard Miracles

On the Road with Magic and Madness

"If you could get rid of yourself just once,
The secret of the secrets would open to you.
The face of the unknown,
Hidden beyond the universe would appear
On the mirror of your perception."
Rumi

I enter an amphitheater that reminds me of one of those 19th century opera houses and slowly make my way down the center aisle. The plush burgundy seats are empty, the lighting soft, and the feel of the place is pitch perfect. I have never been here, and yet the place feels familiar.

I detect the presence of unseen beings emanating pure love. These ascended souls silently guide me down the aisle to take a seat up front. I look directly ahead to an empty stage with polished hardwood floors. After a moment in peaceful reflection, a message is wordlessly communicated:

"You are invited to write a book."

Me... thinking and wondering... A couple beats pass. "I am?"

I look again toward the stage and a bright display of lights, like something you might see on a Broadway marquis, slowly illuminates one word at a time … *Hitchhiking with Larry David – A True Story.*

A smile comes to my face, as a wellspring of memories and scenes washes gently over me, then a slight laugh at some of the summer's absurdities, followed by a thought. "Well, I *did* hitchhike with Larry."

The unseen ascended souls pour forth upon me a warm flowing energy that cascades through the essence of my being. Something is transmitted. I look down on my form glowing and pulsating with a muted light.

I feel the energy of the gift penetrate the layers of my being and slowly seep into the depths of my soul.

"*You* are invited to write a book."

"Invited, not commanded?"

"*Infinite Love would never command anything.*"

I take a moment to look around the large theater searching for the loving beings interacting with me … yet… I see only empty seats.

"May I ask where I am?"

"*Someplace between here and there. You come here often, but this time you shall remember.*"

As I soak up the luminous energy of my surroundings, my glowing form grows brighter and more expansive. "Thank you."

"*We are honored to serve. Go now and walk in peace.*"

I see a silhouette of a hand on my chest, which intensifies my radiance. I feel a soft pair of lips kissing my right cheek. The feeling within me is now intensifying. Though my eyes are closed, I see a bright light next to me. I suddenly seem more dense and earthly, as I become aware of my breath.

"Pauly, wake up. You're having a dream."

I open my eyes and see the Miracle in all her glory, pressed against me, her warm hand on my heart.

She is smiling as she says, "Good morning."

I put my arm around her neck and gently kiss her cheek. "Good morning, angel. Where am I?"

"In bed with me on a perfect September morning in the Vineyard."

As I watch the breeze blow the curtains through the window in our room, I let her words sink in and the logistics of my moment begin to amble back to me: I'm on the island with the Miracle. This is the last day of our two-week reconnection experience; we return to Nashville tonight and start our second-chance dance.

"Miracle, are you actually here, or is this a dream?"

She gives me another soft kiss, and whispers, "This is real, my love. What was your dream about?"

It takes me a moment to get my bearings since both realities appear to be true. "Something transcendent just asked—or rather, invited—me to write a book."

She chuckles. "Really?"

"Yes."

"Pauly, do you remember the theme?"

"Hitchhiking with Larry David."

She laughs softly. "Of course. After all, he did pick you up."

As the soft white sheets rest on top of us, I consider the dream and ponder the invitation of the book. "Miracle, I wonder if I can write a book."

She leans in, kisses my neck, then pulls back and looks into me with those luminous green eyes. "I believe you can do anything you want. Remember, you're magical."

Me... Thinking ...

Since the moment we met the Miracle has had this unshakable belief in the Power of Pauly and knows in her cells that I'm headed for impressive things.

Her breath blows gently against my neck. "Do you remember the long walk we took on the beach on our second date?"

"Yes, in Del Mar. We ended up spending sixteen hours together, and when you drove away, I felt like we *still* didn't have enough time."

"Pauly, on that walk I told you that you have a destiny and are here to help people."

"Miracle, no one has ever believed in me so passionately."

She sits up, exposing her stunning, naked form and picks up a bottle of water from the antique nightstand. Her olive skin is bronzed by the past two weeks of glorious late summer weather. The two of us have spent endless hours on the Vineyard's pristine beaches swimming and basking in the glory of the island.

"Girl, your natural beauty still takes my breath away."

She blushes slightly. "Oh, Pauly." The Miracle gets quiet, looks out into the distance as if receiving a transmission and then turns to me, saying, "I also told you on that trek that you are going to write a book."

"And I said, somewhat stunned, a book?"

She laughs. "Pauly, you need to trust me on this stuff. Listen to the angels ... and of course, me."

"Miracle, I didn't know there was a difference."

Chapter 1

"The first time ever I saw your face
I thought the sun rose in your eyes
And the moon and the stars were the gifts you gave
To the dark and the endless skies"
Ewan MacColl

The next morning we awake in our cozy Nashville townhouse. While the Miracle showers and gets ready for work, I head into the kitchen to make us a couple of lattes.

I look out the French doors and watch a variety of birds take turns flittering to our feeder. The hardwood floors feel cool on my bare feet as the smell of fresh espresso drifts out of the machine and fills the room.

A few minutes later she emerges in full splendor. I gaze upon her and open my arms. "My Lord, you look resplendent in that black dress. What time is the modeling shoot?"

She smiles. "My biggest fan."

My mind drifts back to that moment four years ago in Del Mar when she waltzed into my life with her flowing, sun-streaked hair and a smile that could melt a wall of ice. She was a friend of a friend-a chance encounter at a dinner party that almost didn't happen— that changed my life forever.

From the beginning there existed an inexplicable familiarity. In the magical moment of our first embrace, I whispered, "Holding you feels like coming home."

"Pauly, are you daydreaming?" She comes in close for a long hug and kisses my neck.

"I was remembering the night we met."

"You are such a hopeless romantic."

"Call me a *hopeful* romantic. You do look fabulous."

"Thank you. I want to make a good impression on my first day."

"The new job begins. I better put a sandwich in your Kim Kardashian lunchbox."

She laughs and squeezes me tighter.

I breathe in her fragrance. "Holding you *still* feels like coming home."

"You do remember our first night together."

The Miracle looks at me like a small child gazing up at a Ferris wheel for the first time. "Did you make me my special latte?"

"Of course." I hand her a cup of black gold. "This is your specially concocted elixir of happiness, guaranteed to kill any morning grouchies."

"Yummy. You take such good care of me." After a long sip of the brew, she checks her hair in the mirror. "I hardly slept, worrying about my first day of work."

"Miracle, between your excellent people skills and supermodel looks, you're a natural for this kind of work."

She gives me a kiss on the cheek. "Thanks for the moral support. Pauly, can you drive me over? I don't want to be late."

Since we have downsized to a single Prius, I shift hats from barista to chauffeur. "At your service, My Lady."

The half-mile trip to the mall takes a quick five minutes and because it feels like the first day of school, I walk her inside.

She is the new manager of the Sunglass Shack, with a corporate mandate to sell as many cheaply-made yet exorbitantly-priced pieces of plastic to what Noam Chomsky compassionately calls "the bewildered herd."

After a kiss farewell, I give her a hug and then take a lap around the energy-draining vortex of synthetic light.

Before escaping I sneak a peek at my girl... looking quite dear in her tiny retail fiefdom. I marvel that the fates brought us back together, and at how far we have come from our embryonic days strolling the beaches in Del Mar.

In my head I hear her voice, *"Pauly, you can do it."*

I reach into my pocket and take out a small, crumpled piece of paper. I'd scribbled "Hitchhiking with Larry David" on it the morning before, post-dream.

A spontaneous chuckle pops out of me as I consider the absurdity of the summer. A woman walks by and gives me a strange look, perhaps wondering what this fool is laughing about to himself.

Can I write a book? Why not start and see what happens?

Back at the house, I find an old yellow pad and initiate a primitive outline by recalling as many of the summer's surreal moments as possible: Larry picking me up, my parent's craziness, the beauty of the Vineyard, and of course my Miracle reunion.

Opening up my laptop, I take a shot at writing. To my surprise, the words come in waves, and then keep coming.

Ten hours later, still going strong, my flow is interrupted by a world-weary voice on the phone. "Pauly, I am finally done. Can you come get me? I am so tired, and my feet are killing me. Help me..."

It takes me all of twenty minutes to retrieve her and put those tired, aching toes in my hands. I slowly attempt to rub from them all the retail hell and agony they have absorbed. "How does that feel?"

"Heavenly…" Her face contorts. "Oh, right there… okay, not so firm. I don't know if I can do this forty to fifty hours a week."

I get up and close the blinds.

"Pauly, do you mind pouring me a glass of wine? I need to unwind and forget about all the pain in my body."

"Is white alright?"

She smiles, and I open up a bottle and pour her a glass.

She takes it from me. "Thank you." After a long, slow sip, "My God, that is so good."

I glance down at her pair of super-high black heels. "Speaking of God, I don't think she intended human beings to stand in those kind of shoes. But I do think you should wear them to bed tonight…"

She laughs.

"Seriously girl, why not get a pair of flats or cool black sneakers that are way more comfortable?

The Miracle looks at me as if I had just suggested setting the neighbor's Labrador on fire. "Are you kidding? I can't wear flats. You have to wear hot, sexy shoes. You have to look glamorous."

"Is that the company's rule?"

"The unspoken rule." She takes another sip of her Sauvignon Blanc and relaxes back into the oversized leather chair. "Besides, those shoes make my ass look better."

"Well then, say no more..!"

Classified Information: There is a top-secret bachelor maxim: "Beware any woman in super-crazy shoes. The crazier the shoes, the crazier the gal." I ponder this a moment before returning to my role of in-house reflexologist.

"Pauly, this feels so good. Thank you." She puts her glass down and leans forward to deliver a sweet little kiss on my lips."

I smile. "I'm well paid."

She takes a deep breath. "The district manager was training me, so I never had a moment to call you. We didn't even take a lunch break. The minutiae is mind-boggling." She takes another sip and lets go of a deep exhale. "Oh my God, your hands feel heaven-sent."

"Maybe I missed my calling as a manservant."

"Your hands are so strong."

"Probably from all of those years of playing the piano. Certainly not from any manual labor."

She grins and I feel my stomach respond in joy. "Pauly what did you do all day?"

"Well, I started the book. Or more accurately, I started a Word document."

Her face glows. "You did? That's thrilling! I love the thought of you writing."

She looks down at her feet, then into my eyes, then away, and back again. "God, I so missed you this past summer. It was tough to be apart."

I suddenly feel completely emptied out.

Flashback~

She is gone.

Our townhouse is empty and silent, and I feel gutted. The sleepless nights drift by with faded stars turning into weary sunrises. Food has lost its taste as I stagger through an endless series of zombie days.

She is gone.

Since people keep asking me why the band broke up, I avoid our favorite haunts and the burden of repeating the same sad story for the curious and the caring.

So this is what I wanted?

When I did the clean sweep and got rid of all the drama and madness, I also cast out the love and connection. Yet there is no peace in this stark landscape devoid of laughter, touch, and tenderness.

She is gone.

To be still is to feel intense pain. To move is to feel numb. So I wander like a ghost throughout the deserted city where late night yellow lights flash caution to anyone silly enough to still be casting about. I roam these darkened streets long after everything rational is closed. I drive for hours while every sane soul is in bed ensconced within the arms of his beloved.

To disregard love feels like a sin and the ultimate form of self-destruction.

Heavens, what have I done?

She is gone.

~~~

"Pauly, where did your mind go? I was saying how hard it was to be separated."

I squeeze her feet gently and exhale. "You have no idea."

"But that is behind us now." She smiles warmly.

"Amen." I put my arms around her and press her against me gently.

She kisses my cheek. "Come to bed with me."

Chapter 2

"We delight in the beauty of the butterfly,
But rarely admit the changes it has gone through
To achieve that beauty."
Maya Angelou

Oh sweet Nashville, the Athens of the south. Twenty years ago, I arrived in town with three hundred bucks in my pocket, a bunch of songs under my arm, and stars in my eyes.

The one thing that distinguishes Music City is the warmth and kindness of the people.

The town is a good mix of just big enough and not too large. Nashville also has a huge church about every thirty feet. I once counted over two hundred First Baptist Church franchises, leading me to propose a linear number system to avoid the inevitable confusion.

"Hey, where do you go to church?"

"#236 Baptist Church, how about you?"

"#129 Baptist on Wood Avenue."

"#129? Brother, they don't understand Jesus. Only we do."

In fact, Music City has the most churches per capita in America and "where do you attend services" is a common question, mostly among people with a higher ratio of polyester to cotton in their closets.

When religious folks ask me, "Have you ever been saved?"

I can always sincerely answer, "Yes, once off the coast of Martha's Vineyard by two women on a surfboard."

The best seasons here are spring and fall. Summer is the worst, with its withering heat, a ton of humidity, and an over-abundance of country music fans.

Like many others, I never planned on staying long, but Nashville, with its ease and subtle Southern charm, has a way of growing on you.

I lived for years just outside the city on a few acres of land with a small pack of freeloading dogs. But when I sold my entertainment business and the last of the dogs moved on, I began living the new paradigm of less is more.

The Miracle and I eventually settled on a sweet two-story townhouse in the heart of town, allowing easy walking access to all kinds of cool places.

On this beautiful fall afternoon, she and I take a stroll over to our favorite Mexican restaurant for a late lunch. While enjoying bites of chips and salsa, I notice my phone light up with a name from the past. "Hey Love, it's Peter Pan."

"Pauly, take it," she says.

I press the accept button. "Peter P, what a pleasant surprise."

A sad and broken voice comes forth. "Hey, brother. I'm sorry to call you out of the blue, but I had to share. It's over."

"Over?"

"Yes. After ten years of marriage, the Little Gypsy and I are breaking up. I'm coming back to Nashville. I feel lost. I'm not sure what to do."

I put my hand over the phone and mouth to the Miracle, "He's getting a divorce and coming back to town."

Without hesitation she whispers, "Invite him to stay with us."

"Hey, brother, why don't you stay at our place until you figure things out. You can have the whole upstairs."

"Do you still have your big home in the woods?"

"No, I sold that albatross. We live in Green Hills. It's five minutes from everything."

"How kind ... are you sure? I'd hate to get in your way. But I do need a place to land. Man, I can't believe it's over. My God."

If there ever was the sound of heartbreak, it was there in Peter Pan's words.

"Please stay with us. Even under these circumstances, it'll be a treat to see you."

"Okay. Maybe for a few nights. Thanks."

"When do you think you'll be in Nashville?"

"Sometime tomorrow in the early evening. Hey, I appreciate this. I probably only need a couple of days before I head back. This can't be the end. We have to work this out. We can't throw away ten years."

We hang up and I gaze across the table. "It looks like his marriage is ending. He will be here tomorrow."

She frowns, "How sad. But maybe it's just a bump in the road for them. Pauly, do you remember the dinner the four of us shared at the big house on the water in Del Mar?"

I reflect for a moment, "Yes. I think that was my third day in town and our second day together." The waiter comes over and clears a few plates from the table.

She takes a sip of her iced tea. "Well, we weren't technically together but it sure felt like we had already joined as one. Peter and his wife were in the next town over visiting her family, right?"

"Yes. Without planning it we all ended up leaving Nashville and visiting San Diego for the holidays." The waiter returns and fills my water, then leaves the check

13

on the table. "Miracle, how ironic that we just reunited and they are going apart."

"That is crazy and tragic. I hope they can work things out. How did you and Peter meet?"

"I met Peter Pan in Nashville about ten years ago through his wife, the Little Gypsy. He was this petite fellow who was light in his step, quick with his wit, and California dirty blond handsome. We had a nice rapport immediately." I place some cash on the table then turn back toward my lovely companion.

"Unfortunately, our past was marred and scarred by my one and only venture into the exciting world of multilevel marketing."

~~~

A MLM Flashback~

As a public service to the unfamiliar, I will briefly explain how multilevel marketing (MLM) works.

In a multilevel marketing pyramid scheme business model, under the best-case scenario you experience a small to moderate rise of income over a very short period of time, followed by substantial loss of lifetime friendships over a long period time.

Most vital to your instant riches is a 'super special' product that is unattainable through normal retail outlets. In my particular case it was the 'Magical Purple Juice TM'

Now, when you drank the Purple Juice, there definitely was a boost of energy followed by a brief period of general well being. Perhaps this had something to do with the crazy amount of stimulants contained within the drink. Or, perhaps, as the company propaganda myth promised, it was the secret blend of exotic herbs and ingredients.

Of course, like all MLM products, the expense was a tad prohibitive: like $70 for about 32 oz. (hey, don't you *think you're worth it?). But if you were willing to sign up for the lifetime supply plan, which included all kinds of useless free pamphlets promoting the product and company, you could get it for $59.9995 (Plus shipping, handling, more handling, and up-charges).*

Better still, if you were willing to jeopardize every essential relationship in your life, and pressure soon-to-be-former friends to enlist in the Your Lifetime & Beyond Plan, then you could, in theory, get your "Magical Purple Juice TM" for free! (Plus shipping, handling, more handling, and up-charges.)

If you wanted to feel even more multilevel happiness, you were strongly encouraged to attend a constant and never-ending series of pep rallies. Here various folks who had never quite found their place in life (and maybe did a little prison time) endlessly extolled the virtues of the company. (But only this particular organization, since all the other MLMs are inherently evil and a serious threat to mankind).

By remarkable coincidence, every 'MLM Leader' got into the company for the exact same reason: they simply wanted to help mankind feel better about their lives. Of course it was also nice to build a business that would free them from actually working. (As well as from the burden of any lifelong friendships.)

~~~

The following day, as a gorgeous golden sunset slowly spreads across the Tennessee sky, a road-weary Peter Pan rings our doorbell.

"Welcome, kind sir." I give him a long hug. "Is this all you have, a single bag?"

"That's it. Man, am I beat. That is one hell of a drive all the way from Idaho."

"Well you have come to the end of your long day's night." I take his coat and point up the staircase. "The upstairs is all yours, so pick out a room."

A couple hours later, he wanders down and collapses on the oversized sofa to join us.

"Here, have some hot tea." I hand him a mug. "Did you take a nap?"

He takes a seat, bites on the top of his lip, and then takes a long, slow sip of tea. "No, we just spent three hours on the phone and I have no clue where we are in all of this. I'm a friggin' wreck. Yesterday, I spontaneously broke down on a friend's driveway and couldn't stop crying." He lowers his eyes. "I just lay there on the cold concrete, weeping, in the fetal position. Ten years ..."

Peter Pan shakes his head. "It still feels so strange to be here and not with her." He takes another sip of tea and then sags. "Guys I don't mean to be rude but I am absolutely exhausted..."

She jumps in. "Of course you are. Go upstairs and get some sleep. Pauly will make you one of his famous lattes in the morning." We all hug and he wearily climbs the stairs.

The next morning, I drop off our resident Sunglass Queen at work and return home to the sound of Peter Pan tickling the ivories.

I walk over behind him and put my hand on his shoulder. "Brother, that sounds heavenly." The music fills the room and echoes through the house. "I've known you for years yet never knew you played. I thought you were a guitar player."

Peter nods. "That's my main instrument but I really love the keyboard. Boy, this is a fabulous piano. Pauly, do you still play professionally?"

"It's been light years since I supported myself musically."

He changes songs. "Ten years ago I moved here to write and record music, but got distracted chasing after the Little Gypsy and trying to make her dreams come true. So I never gave it a good shot. But I don't blame her; it's my own fault."

"Did the music bring you back to town?"

"Yes, that's part of it. And, for reasons I can't explain, I felt like I had to see you."

"You're not planning on pitching me any new multilevel marketing ventures?"

He laughs. "How insane. I hope you can forgive me for that one, but the Little Gypsy was so into it I felt like I had to dive in and participate or get divorced. How crazy. Those meetings ..."

"I still have Vietnam-like flashbacks."

He laughs. "Thanks for cheering me up." He starts playing a haunting ballad.

It's lovely. "What an enchanting melody ... but I can't place it."

"Oh thanks! This is one of mine. It's called, *'When Love Finds You.'*" He grins, eyes on the keys."

Later in the morning, after Peter Pan comes and goes past me several times as I labor on my manuscript, he finally asks, "What are you working on?"

"I'm trying to write something that might become a book."

"May I take a look?"

I think about it for a moment or two. Should I share whatever this is with someone? "Well, why not. I'll send you a couple of chapters."

A few hours later, I wander out to find all of the forwarded material printed and marked up with what turn out to be excellent suggestions.

Peter Pan comes flying in, as he is apt to do. "It's great. However, you have a long way to go."

"Thank you. Man, there are a lot of marks."

He chuckles. "Have you ever considered using grammar? It might help."

"I knew I should have finished high school." I focus down on a few specific comments. "This is very helpful; where did you learn these skills?"

"I used to be an editor."

"No... I thought you produced television programs."

"Yes, for years, but I also spent some time as a copy editor."

"I had no idea. Peter Pan, you never cease to amaze. Hey, are you headed back to Idaho?"

He shakes his head. "Not after the last phone call. Plus, I think she has already found someone new. It's impossible for her to be alone. Even for five minutes."

Peter Pan looks out the window and then at me. "Since you're being generous enough to let me live here, why don't I help you edit your piece? We could work a couple of hours every morning until I decide to split."

"Are you sure? I hold up the pages of his notes. "It could be a lot of heavy lifting."

"Absolutely. Count me in."

Over the next few days, and then weeks, we sit across from each other with our laptops in front of us at the dining room table and do our thing. Peter Pan and I settle into a deeply transformative literary-emotional process, though my inability to figure out the laws of language continually drives the poor guy batty.

In mock anger, he screeches across the table, "Why can't you remember any of these comma rules? Didn't you read the grammar book I bought you?"

"I did, but nothing sticks."

"I'm going to buy one of those dart guns, and every time you put a comma in the wrong place... pop!"

"Don't even joke about that. We used to play with those as kids and my mom would scream, 'You're not going to be happy until you put an eye out.' Go figure."

Peter Pan, sensing I am throwing out a straight line, dutifully plays along, "So what happened?"

I pretend to ponder Peter's query, "I never did put an eye out but, come to think of it, I haven't ever been truly happy either..."

He shakes his head. "You really are an idiot savant." His smile suddenly vanishes and he glances out of one of the ceiling-to-floor windows that surround us.

A saddened Peter Pan offers, "Why can't my love with her simply work?"

"The million dollar question that no one ever has an answer for." I get up and go into the kitchen, shuffle through a few drawers, and find an old key. "Here, take this and go outside and turn the lock."

He pops up and takes the key. "Okay. Does it work?"

"You'll see."

I lock him out, and he repeatedly tries the key with no luck. "Hey, let me in."

Opening the door, I ask him, "What did you observe?"

"It sort of fits, but it doesn't work." Our eyes meet. "Just like me and her."

"Yes."

I soon discover in Peter Pan the most wonderful friend, a true brother from another mother with gifts that fill the vast empty spaces of my own limitations.

Chapter 3

"Vulnerability is not about fear,
grief and disappointment.
It is the birthplace of everything we are hungry for."
Brene Brown

It is the middle of a cool October evening. As our bodies press tightly together, the Miracle whispers, "Let me get even closer."

I take a long, slow drink of her essence. "This feels heavenly. There is something deeply healing about being held. I remember some long, lonely years before you came along. Miracle, I am so grateful we are back together."

Her whisper is a breath on my chest. "I'm here."

"Thankfully. Do you ever wake up in the middle of the night and feel totally alone in the world? So alone in the Universe?"

"I used to, all the time." She sighs. "But even as a child, I knew you were out there somewhere, and you loved me. It kept me going in some of my darkest days. It made me stronger. I know I can overcome anything. But back then ... having the hope of a 'you,' the hope of an us, was a light in my darkness."

She kisses me. "I love you. I feel we were always connected, and all of the other people before you were simply placeholders. I was waiting for you to come find me."

"When we met, there were all these crazy-rich guys wining and dining you. Part of me never felt good enough; you deserved some wealthy husband with billions of dollars."

"I could have had that many times, but it's you I want to be with. I want real love, not the lonely life so many girls think they want. Maybe if we hadn't met, I would have gone that way. But you changed my paradigm so I could never go back. Pauly, you spoiled me."

"Please don't ever let me go. I don't want to go back to sleeping alone with just a pillow and cold sheets for company."

"You don't have to, love."

Another breath fills me and I release it in a slow sigh. "I always felt like a freak of sorts, having never bought into it all."

"Bought in?"

"You know, the way most people do: the marriage, the house, the kids, the jobs, the routine. For some reason I never swam all the way into the net."

She gently squeezes my arms and I feel her warm breath upon my skin. "You love to be free."

"Yes, that can be a wonderful thing, but sometimes the loneliness can be excruciating. Funny, if you have just one person, one soul, who totally believes in you, the world is so much smaller and less cold. Just one..."

She gives me another little squeeze. I return it and go on. "And there's another kind of emancipation: the freedom to be yourself. These past few years, as I wandered far and wide, with unlimited freedom, I came to understand this sort of intense intimacy. Through shared transparency and authentic interaction, it is perhaps the highest state we can attain. We have this gift."

"It is a gift, a precious thing." She is completely melted against me in heavenly union. Then her voice whispers softly, "I always felt a certain aloneness my whole life, until I met you that night, and then it vanished. Look, Pauly, it is three thirty three."

We shift around and I spoon her. "I love the way you feel, sweet girl."

Chapter 4

Then the Grinch thought of something
he hadn't before!
"Maybe Christmas," he thought,
"Doesn't come from a store."
"Maybe Christmas...perhaps...
means a little bit more!"
Dr. Seuss

As the solstice heralds the arrival of winter, the Miracle makes, by society's standards, a very reasonable request. "Pauly, can we celebrate Christmas?"

Though never a fan of any Madison Avenue-inspired holiday clumsily designed for us to *Buy Random Things We Don't Need*, I decide to meet the Miracle in the middle.

"Well, why not?"

Her suddenly beaming face seems both pleased and shocked. "You agreed so quickly... with gifts and everything?"

"I don't need any presents, but I am more than happy to buy you something from the mall to celebrate the birth of Mr. Jesus."

She picks up her purse off the kitchen table. "Can we go get a tree right now?"

"Sure, but before we dive into all this, I want to pull out some advice from my old friend Dave Ramsey."

"*The Financial Peace* guy on the radio and television who hates debt?"

"Exactly. He once told me, when dealing with a holiday, you and your partner must agree upon a budget and stick to it. Otherwise it is easy to spend a lot more than you can afford and wind up on January 1st with a credit card hangover. Are you fine with a fixed number?"

"Of course. How much should we say?"

I take a look out the window and up into the grey December sky, then across the backyard. The trees have lost their leaves and look barren. It's been years since I celebrated Christmas so for a moment I am at a loss as to what amount is reasonable. "How about $500? Or... let's say $600 including the tree and decorations."

"Deal!" She puts down her purse and gives me a hug. "Pauly, let's go get a tree right now."

An hour later the floor of our living room is covered with the fragrant, horizontal carcass of a Scots Pine. "Miracle, do you have any idea what a dead tree has to do with the birth of the Messiah?"

She shakes her head. "No teasing, Pauly; we are celebrating Christmas."

"But, but..."

Once the tree is propped up, we visit the local five and dime store which supplies us with a wide bevy of lights, decorations, and an eerie electric angel who sits hauntingly atop our ax-murdered tree.

In a noble effort to take the festivities to the next level, I light up the fake-looking gas fireplace and put on Nat King Cole's gold standard Christmas CD.

Our holiday hijinks soon rouse the curiosity of Peter Pan. With a Grinch-like smirk he comes bounding down the stairs to survey the situation and whispers to me, "Are you of all people buying into all this seasonal madness?"

I motion to the oblivious, feverishly decorating Miracle. "Well, when you have children..."

26

With a slight cock of his head and a raised eyebrow Mr. Pan lets me know all he has to say about this.

Since Peter seems a tad skeptical I assure him (and maybe me too) with the details of our holiday agreement. "Don't worry. All this chaos is actually under control. See, we even set a budget."

He gives me another raised eyebrow. "Did she agree to that budget?"

"She did and, in fact, is completely onboard with the amount."

"I hope there is a provision for overruns, my friend." He then begins his ascent up the stairs and I hear him laugh just before he enters his room.

This gives me a moment's pause, but I decide to trust the process and focus instead on the Miracle's yuletide joy.

As the day we have randomly chosen to celebrate the birth of Mr. Jesus approaches, the hallowed ground beneath our murdered tree begins to swell with more and more gifts. Since I only bought her a couple of things, this material overflow leaves me fiscally confused.

So what are in the other twenty-plus boxes with my name on them? Remember to trust the process and enjoy the season. Oh, yes. I got it.

A few days later, I catch my girl dropping off a couple more elaborately wrapped boxes on the five and dime snow. I touch base with her and make sure we are still on the same yuletide fiscal plan. "There certainly are a lot of presents here."

She gazes upon the colored lights and the creepy swirling Christmas Angel. "Yes, doesn't it all look so sparkly?"

"And are we staying within our agreed upon $600 budget?" I motion to the piles of boxes under the green corpse.

"I may end up going over a couple of dollars, but for the most part, yes. I think you're going to love all of your gifts. Do you like the angel on top?"

"To be honest, it sort of reminds me of something from one of those *Twilight Zone* episodes where the spooky thing comes to life and kills all the people in the house. Not to be superstitious, but maybe when we go to bed, we should start locking our door. At least until we take the tree to the recycling center."

She chuckles. "This is all so idyllic."

A couple days later there are even more presents marked for me under the tree as Peter Pan and I sit on the overstuffed couch and sip some tea in front of the admittedly-lovely-but-soon-to-be-a-pile-of-wood-chips Scots Pine and try to make some sense of Christmas.

I go first. "Call me ignorant, but I am having the hardest time connecting the Prince of Peace to all this mindless consumption and dead trees filled with lights." The strange spinning creepy angel suddenly offers an evil sideways glance, stops, and appears to become annoyed with me. I point at the top of the tree. "Hey, did you see that?"

"See what?"

I glance at the creepy angel one more time then continue. "This morning when I dropped the Miracle at the mall, there wasn't a whole lot of unconditional love flowing around the parking lot. One day soon, the Sermon on the Mount will probably be called the Sermon at the Mall."

Peter Pan shakes his head. "Or I can hear a prayer starting with 'Our Father who art at Wal-Mart...' It's insane."

I get up and put some more hot water in my cup before coming back to the sofa. "Is it me, or has America gone crazy?"

"I'm with you, brother. I find the whole thing just repugnant." He looks up. "Man, you're right. Your tree angel is kind of creepy."

"Don't piss it off. I'm a bit frightened by it."

He laughs. "Well, the Miracle seems to be having a good time with it all." Peter Pan sweeps his hand toward the mountain of gifts covering the fake snow under the tree. "How's the budget coming?"

I wince. "At her request, I've resisted looking online at the debit card balance 'so I don't ruin the surprise' she intends, but unless a lot of these boxes are full of old newspapers, I'm probably in for a different kind of shock. I must admit I have enjoyed seeing her so enthralled with the whole holiday season."

He looks serious for a moment. "It probably helps to take her mind off her job."

"Exactly, and her aching feet." He gets up, grabs a box and hands it to me. I hold it for a moment and then pass it back." Let's hope that whatever is in all these boxes is easily returnable."

Peter Pan puts the box back and moves around a few other presents. "Some of these for you are kind of heavy." He picks up one rather large, beautifully wrapped and shiny package. "This one even feels pricey. What do you think she bought you?"

"A handmade Irish wool-hunting outfit."

Peter looks puzzled. "But you don't even hunt."

I raise my hands. "My point exactly. By the way, I can see you are getting quite a kick out of my merry madness."

He chuckles. "Is it that obvious?" He puts the gift down. "Good luck, my friend." He pats my shoulder and floats back upstairs to his bedroom cave.

Later in the evening, the Miracle comes home with a few more presents and the look of a rabid animal.

Could she be possessed by the Creepy Christmas Angel? Should I check to see if she is running a fever? Cautiously I inquire, "Are you all right, my love?"

"I'm loving this Christmas! Thank you so much for doing this."

I hug her and then look into her eyes. "Remember honey, I don't need anything, and you don't have to get me a lot of stuff. Being with you is my gift."

"Pauly, I love buying presents for you! This is my way of saying thank you. Gifts are one of my love languages."

"But remember that having sex with you is MY love language."

She either misses my jest, or is in a Christmas trance. She spends the next hour rearranging the presents just so and organizing the ornaments, all under the watchful eye of the eerily spinning, definitely evil Creepy Christmas Angel.

When the big day finally arrives, life blesses us with a light snowfall that turns our property into a pristine white landscape. We share a couple of smoothies and settle in on the nice, soft sofa. I must admit a part of me feels guilty because I only got her four or five things. She wants to open her packages first and is gracious and appreciative of the things I selected for her.

Now it's my turn.

The gifts are well thought out and obviously selected with love and care. The only problem is there are so many of them: an expensive camera, cashmere

30

sweaters and wool pants, a couple of ties (ok, not all of the gifts were well-selected). There are a couple hundred bucks worth of tea from Teavana, a beige pair of leather loafers, and a whole lot of more, more, more...

There is no way all this bounty costs anywhere close to $600 (the tree alone was $80 and I spent $200) so...

What do I do? What do I say? I don't want to ruin Christmas, but I don't want to have to go to work at Wal-Mart to pay for Christmas.

After a short walk around the neighborhood to admire the lovely morning, the Miracle jumps into the shower and I pop on the computer to see how much this holiday adventure has cost.

When I finally add it all up, the figure sits north of four thousand dollars!

Obviously, my desire to inculcate a sense of financial responsibility has failed. I sit there in shock. I need the ghost of Dave Ramsey to show up like Jacob Marley and restore some sanity. I suddenly feel like I am in business with M.C. Hammer.

Worse, the Creepy Christmas Angel is sitting above me with an evil smile, gloating.

Chapter 5

"The bond that links your true family
Is not one of blood,
But of respect and joy in each other's life,
Rarely do members of one family
Grow up under the same roof."
Richard Bach, Illusions:
The Adventures of a Reluctant Messiah

On the first morning of March I sit on the back deck and watch a butterfly gently move between psychedelic-colored flowers. The vast ambit of the natural world floods over me, from this tiny creature to the raw power of a tornado. What mystery holds it all together?

A lone cloud slowly passes above, giving witness to all that lies below. Though winter has not yet officially departed, the morning is cool and brisk. I close my eyes and the let the warm rays of the sun penetrate my being.

My phone rings. "Hello."

A gentle voice on the end softly says, "Well, how is my son?"

"Ah, father..."

I hear him take a deep breath. "Well, I had not spoken to you since you left the Vineyard back in September, which is what, almost six months? God, the time flies, and well, I just wanted to make sure you were okay. Are you doing alright?"

This was a highly unusual unfolding. Dad never calls. You ring him, so part of me is caught off guard. "Yes, things are fine here. Is everything going well?"

"There's no news. Your mother and I are good. How about you; how is Nashville?"

It feels as if we are taking slow baby steps as we try to connect. "Spring is approaching, it's getting warmer, we are buoyant, and our lives are pretty low-key."

"How is your girl?"

"How kind of you to ask. She's managing a sunglass store down at the mall. How's Mom?"

"The same. We are watching a lot of old movies, doing our crossword puzzles, walking Max. I was just concerned because we had not heard from you in so long, which is unusual."

Now I take a deep breath. Should I be real or keep things on the surface? I dip a toe in the water. "Well, after the strain between us the past summer, I just thought it would be wise to be respectful and give you some space."

There's a deafening silence on the line. "You can't take your old man's insanity and craziness seriously. After all this time, you should know this. You're a good kid and we love you."

"Thank you, Dad. This means a lot."

"Maybe next summer you two can come stay at the cabin for awhile. I would like to see you and for us to spend some time together."

Did Dad really just say that? Last year he appeared annoyed by my very presence. I wonder what caused this shift?

"Dad, what a nice offer. Maybe we can make that happen."

"I hope we can." He takes a deep breath. "I'd also like to say... last summer I was kind of... it wasn't really you, you see... I was just feeling..." He takes another deep breath. "Well, I better go make your mother breakfast. I love you. I'm glad I took the time to call."

"Thank you, Dad. I'm touched you did and I love you too."

Click.

As the morning slowly warms up, I sit there and ponder Dad's call. Though short, it feels like an unexpected gift left outside my door. This is an invitation, an opening, and certainly something to be explored.

A sparrow lands a few feet away and serenades me briefly with a song before flying off. Despite the pain of the past, if my Dad reaches out to me in reconciliation, I have to reach back. You can't give up on people, no matter how hard it gets.

Peter Pan sticks his head out the door, "Let's get to work."

"Give me a minute here to shift gears." I run to the bathroom and throw some water on my face. I grab a glass of orange juice and put on some hot water for tea.

Peter watches me in the kitchen. "Are you done stalling?"

"Is it that obvious?"

"Well, it happens every day. I've gotten used to it. Come on lazy bones; let's finish this bit about The Ted Danson Principle. Go ahead and read me what you have."

I come back to the table and look down at my paper and begin. "I get out and walk straight up the steps of the Chilmark Store and into the warm smile of My Savior Ted. We exchange greetings, and keeping my priorities in order, (1) Pizza (2) Famous People, I go inside to get my piece of the proverbial pie."

Peter laughs, "That's funny. Keep going."

"Thanks. You don't think the whole me eating thing is getting worn out?"

He thinks for a moment, puts his pen in his mouth, then says, "Not really, because it was a big part of your summer routine."

I make a note, and then continue. "When I return to the porch, My Savior Ted surprises me. "Are you on your own?"

"Yes I am. Are you?"

"Yes. Mary's out of town. Would you like to join me for lunch?"

"I would love to." (The big meeting at last! A famous person likes me!). Peter, do you think I need to add Mary's last name so they know she is a well-known actress?"

"Will people know the name Mary Steenburgen? I doubt that matters, and we don't want to slow the story down, but I think it's good you are paying more attention to details. Never assume the reader knows anything."

"Or more importantly the writer."

Peter smiles and shakes his head. "This is especially true of you, Mr. Idiot Savant. Now keep going."

I look for my place on the page. "About midway through our meal, I realize there is no agenda lurking in my back pocket. I'm just here with a wonderful guy, sharing an interesting conversation. Stripped of any expectation or pretense, our encounter is free to unfold organically. And why should our interaction be any different because Ted happens to be on TV? Is that what matters most? Does fame or celebrity give a human being more inherent value? (Actually the answer is yes. According to Wikipedia, a famous person is, on average, two hundred times more valuable than a normal person.)"

In the midst of our groove, my cell phone keeps lighting up. When it goes off a few more times, I know it can only be the Miracle, who won't take a 'no pick up' for an answer.

"Yes, darling?" I say in my best impersonation of an Upper East Side Society Dame.

"Why didn't you pick up?" The grand inquisitor asks.

"We're right in the middle of editing a chapter and I didn't want to lose our momentum. Whazzup?"

"I'm done early; can you come get me?"

"Give me about twenty minutes to finish this thread and I'll pop down to the Church of Consumption and get you."

A half hour later I fetch my lovely cohort from the curb. Once in the car she suggests, "Can we get a movie for tonight and snuggle up on the couch?"

Her movie of choice is usually one of those mindless romantic comedies with a paint-by-numbers script. This runs completely counter to my Mr. Heavy Drama, way-too-complex approach to film viewing.

"Okay, my retail goddess. Hey, I'm craving some grapefruit, so let's stop at Whole Foods, and then pick up the film."

"Do we have to stop at the store? You're probably going to run into fifty people you know and we won't get home for hours. Can't we just go straight back? After this past week at the mall, I am completely fried on people. In fact, I don't even want to stop and try to find a movie. I'm feeling worn out and don't have any energy left."

No movie? This must be serious. "But I am deeply craving some grapefruit...how about if I promise to just run in and run out."

"Pauly..."

We pull into the large parking lot and presto..."Look, there's a spot right in front. It's a sign."

"Well, I am coming in with you to make sure you do not stop and talk to anyone. Pauly, you always need herding." She gives me a sly smile.

With my social shepherd close at hand, I grab the grapefruit, turn the corner, and...

No way!

There, right in front of me, is Ted Danson himself.

Is this a mirage brought on by too much writing? Am I now seeing my literary creations moving about in the world as third dimensional forms?

Then up walks his wife Mary.

So it is him!

Now, I am not a star-struck person and have seen Ted and Mary many times on the Vineyard, but this one throws me for a loop. I mean, I was just editing the Ted Danson section and then, all of a sudden, here he is.

Presto!

They are in Nashville of all places?

Ted Danson of The Ted Danson Principle fame in my backyard?

It takes me a few seconds to process this... Ted is in front of me... I know Ted... But wait, this is not the Vineyard... Editing the section... Ted and Mary here... what are the odds...

HOLY SHIT—!

Unfortunately—for all parties concerned—my metaphysical enthusiasm is not exactly channeled in a healthy, reasonable way (I'm being way too diplomatic here). I approach these two poor carbon-based life forms and let me see... what's a nice way to put it... oh, okay... I FREAK OUT!

"Oh my God!!! Ted!!! Mary!!! This is impossible!!!"

Ted's already leaning back, mouth open.

Mary, ever gracious, smiles slightly. "Hi there, I'm Mary..."

"Oh my God!!! Ted!!! Mary!!! This is impossible!!!"

~~~

My attire: black warm up suit, black ski cap, unshaven...

My demeanor: wild-eyed, half-crazed, incoherent...

Ted's face: *Somebody call the cops!*

Fortunately for me, the Miracle remains placid and sane. Ted probably thinks she's my doctor.

I take off my ski cap and Mary finally recognizes me. "Oh heavens, it's you." She visibly relaxes. "We didn't recognize you." She gives me a hug.

Ted makes a generous and gracious overture to the Miracle. "Hi there, nice to meet you, I'm Ted." He sticks out his hand and they shake.

After a few moments of small talk, I am no longer hyperventilating and am almost coherent. "What brings you both to Nashville?"

Ted says, "This is our first trip here. In fact, we just got off the plane about 45 minutes ago and came straight to the store."

Then Mary. "I've always wanted to write songs and Nashville is the place to be. I'm here for a week to co-write with a number of people. I'm kind of nervous and very excited all at once."

Ted starts stacking his groceries on the checkout stand and asks, without making eye contact, "What are you working on these days?"

"I'm writing a book called *Hitchhiking With Larry David*."

He stops and looks up at me, and wryly smiles. "What a clever title."

"It's a true story. And there is even a section about you in it."

"Interesting." After a moment, "Well, good luck with it."

Ted Probably Thinking: This guy is nuts. Somebody call the cops.

After goodbyes and another hug from Mary, I stagger away.

You have to love Mary. There is something grounded yet angelic about this woman. After sharing any time with her, I always come away feeling better about the world and it's easy to see why Ted feels 'she's the best thing that ever happened to me.' Perhaps someday the Miracle and I will inspire people in the way we love and interact with the world. Perhaps...

The Miracle immediately rides me about my over-the-top behavior. "Oh my God, you were like psycho-man back there. Since when are you star-struck? I have never been so embarrassed."

"I am, too. But what are the odds of my working on his section of the book, taking a break, and running into them an hour after they arrive here in Nashville? This is close to impossible, and that's my defense for freaking out. This whole universal synchronicity thing just blows my mind."

"But stuff like this *always* happens to you. Why do you still seem so surprised?"

"I guess I'm like a dog who always falls for the fake throw or a baby and the game of peek-a-boo. Do you think Ted will ever forgive me?"

She laughs. "Not a chance… you are lucky he didn't call security. Pauly, you are like a little boy. Now let's go home where it's cozy."

Chapter 6

"Look to love you may dream,
And if it should leave then give it wings.
But if such a love is meant to be;
Hope is home, and the heart is free"
Enya

Most mornings start with me rising early and getting on an exercise bike down at the YMCA. Afterward, I unwind by meditating in the steam room. If the conditions are just right, I can expand into a deep theta state. Once refreshed, it's time to return home, awaken the Miracle, play barista, and get to work with Peter Pan.

Today I decide to linger longer in the sauna and allow the heat to penetrate my cells, to clear and cleanse me. The warmth feels heavenly and being here alone is incubating. I meditate for a few minutes, even sing, and then finally pull myself out and into a cold shower.

Upon returning home, I wander into the kitchen and fire up the espresso machine. The Miracle wanders out and I give her a kiss on the forehead. "Someone looks sleepy."

She kisses me back. "Can I have my coffee?"

"Give me paw?"

She wearily trades a long hug for her latte. "Thank you, Pauly. God, I am so tired. I woke up in the middle of the night and could not fall back asleep for a long time."

"How come?"

"There are all these new company policies and I am concerned our store is not towing the line. Plus, my district boss seems out to get me."

"I thought he loved you."

"He did for the first month, but now it feels like everything I do is wrong. I'm worried, Pauly." Her forehead wrinkles and she looks forlorn.

I put an arm around her. "You're too hard on yourself. Relax and just do your best. If it doesn't work out, it's not a big deal. That place is a quick pit stop on a long road."

"Easy for you to say."

"Only because I have already had my espresso. You should hear me when I first wake up."

She shakes her head, smiles and sips from her mug. "This is delicious. What are you doing today besides hitting the gym, writing and hanging out with your buddies at Whole Foods?"

"You left out the part about me telling bad jokes."

"I didn't want to be mean."

"That is very funny my lovely goddess with the cute derriere. I actually have a healing session with my beloved Saint Bonnie. It's been awhile and I need a blast of her good vibes."

"Pauly, I want your life. This isn't fair."

"Life is never fair, little one." I give her a pat on the backside. "What a lovely caboose!"

"My butt is way too big. I want to hang out all day and then go see Bonnie."

"You want to talk to Bonnie about the size of your tush?"

"That's not nice. I need a session too."

I smile and give her a soft hug. "You should, to defrag from the mall. I'll see if she has time this week."

"No, my day off is next Monday. Can you ask Bonnie if she will see me then?"

This surprises me. "I thought you had two days off this week?"

44

"Nope. We have inventory and are introducing a new line of sunglasses. So there is no break for me, Mr. Writer of Words and Phrases. Shoot, look at the time, I'm late. Let me throw on some clothes. I'll do my makeup there."

"No hurry, I'll take you over when you're ready."

Now she seems perturbed. "I wish we had another car; I'm getting tired of you driving me back and forth."

"It's not a problem for me. Besides, the car would just sit at the mall all day and feel lonely."

"Whatever."

After dropping the Miracle off at her job, I head over to Saint Bonnie's humble healing studio for some love. I enter and sit in one of the large soft chairs. Being here takes me back a few years...

~~~

Saint Bonnie Flashback~

My life has come to a place of emotional numbness. I slowly move through the world in a state of detached depression.

'What's the use?'

As a meaningless fragment moving through an indifferent and hostile universe, I could not answer that question.

Did I believe in God?

Not really.

Did I believe in anything?

Just that life was a struggle and the world was a tough place to be.

Through grace and the word of a friend, I wander into Saint Bonnie's world.

I sit across from a middle-aged former nurse who has dedicated her life to helping others. She speaks of angels and masters, but never pretends to understand the vast mystery operating around and through her.

45

"My job is to get out of the way and let the power of God do its work," she says.

A non-believer, I think sarcastically, yeah sure, if you say so.

We start the session sitting opposite each other and sharing before I lay down on her comfortable table.

My cynicism is immediately shattered by an uncanny sensation. "Bonnie, I feel hands all over me."

She whispers softly. "Those are the angels, my son."

I gently drift off to a realm of complete relaxation, peace, and bliss.

My hour on the table feels like two weeks in the tropics. It is nothing short of life-altering! 99.9% of the things I experience transcend language and sharing.

For the next few years I go once, sometimes twice a week. Bonnie is confident that, with the blessing of God's grace, I can be put back together.

~~~

I enter a small room and take my place in one of the two soft upholstered chairs facing each other. Three candles burn on a wooden altar across from me. A few moments later, Saint Bonnie emerges, a touch more gray in her hair than I remember. She greets me with a warm smile and a long hug.

"My dear son, how are you?" I can make out just a trace of her New England roots in her accent.

I smile and look into her brown eyes. "A long way from where you found me."

She laughs. "Oh, I'll say. Come, let's catch up."

"Oh, before I forget: the Miracle would like to see you next Monday for an appointment."

She raises an eyebrow, "Did you two reunite?"

"We did. One could say... quite miraculously."

Her laugh comes easily. "Clever. I'm so happy for the both of you. I know how much love you share. It

46

would be an honor to see her again." She takes a deep breath. "Let's take a moment of silence, shall we?"

And we do.

After a deep breath I say softly, "I have a point of concern, but it's not a major thing."

She suddenly looks more serious and gestures with her hand. "Please, go ahead and share."

I grimace for a moment and scan the room, trying to find my words. "Well, the Miracle and I are experiencing an ever-increasing dissonance around the distinct difference of our daily experience. While I feel like I am following my bliss with this writing project, she's getting blisters on her feet from her job at the mall."

Bonnie doesn't say anything, just motions for me to keep going.

"I spend my days writing and then editing with Peter. Then I go to the gym or meditate. Perhaps have a leisurely lunch with friend or maybe take a walk at the lake for inspiration. During the evening, I have a nice dinner with my Goddess. Life is fabulous."

"Is she paying the bills?"

"Actually we live primarily off my savings, so she can channel her salary towards paying off old debts she accumulated before we met. But there seems to be resentment building, which part of me understands, yet it's still disappointing when it rears its ugly head."

"I'm sure it's tough on the energetic level, too. Remember, you primarily exist in a clear environment at a high level, while she is in the mall, which is full of so much false need. The Miracle is also very sensitive, so she would tend to pick up on a lot on those negative vibrations. It may be tough at times, but I would encourage you to be empathic towards her."

47

"It's hard to see someone you care about suffer. I know it's only temporary."

Bonnie agrees, "Everything is, 'and this too shall pass.' She can use her time there as a practice in presence and peace."

"I'll let you tell her that. By the way, I don't think anyone, even an ascended master, could find peace standing for hours in those ridiculously high heels."

Her laugh comes forth. "An ascended master would never wear them. Why doesn't she buy a nice pair of comfortable shoes?"

I cock my head as if to feign shock. "I thought you were wise; don't you know the importance of the Invisible Fashion Rules?"

She gestures towards her own modest wardrobe, "Obviously not..."

"Apparently you don't, Bonnie. I won't turn you in, but you are not allowed inside the mall for the next six months."

She nods and raises her hands. "Guilty as charged. Okay. No more talk; let's get you on the table so the angels can have a go at you."

"My ethereal rewards await me. Thank you." We then move from one plane of existence to another.

Chapter 7

"A man has got to know his limitations"
Dirty Harry in Magnum Force

The Miracle and I have been invited to a friend's birthday dinner with three other couples at a cute restaurant. At some point during the evening the Miracle turns to me, kisses me on the cheek, and says, "I love nights like this. Thank you, Pauly."

At the end of the soirée everyone hugs with promises made to reunite in revelry. On the short ride home she spontaneously says, "Can we swing by the fern bar near Whole Foods? You know the one where you can sit outside? I want to keep this fabulous evening flowing."

"Sure, why not."

"Thank you. It has been a rough couple work weeks and I just want to relax." She runs her hand up the inside of my leg. "Of course I will really thank you later."

"Promises, promises..."

The night is cool and crisp as we grab a couple of oversized chairs right next to an outdoor fire pit affording us a wonderful view of the stars scattered above us. A waitress takes our order and returns with some champagne for her and a Perrier for me.

We toast the night's beauty.

"To the stars and to us," I say as we touch glasses and then lips.

"Amen. Pauly, tell me the real reason you never drink?"

I ponder my response as I take a sip from my mineral water. "Well, the short answer is I simply don't like it. The taste, the feeling, it never resonated with me. Though I did get sloshed once."

She laughs. "Tell me about it."

I shake my head. "I think I was fourteen. I was scheduled to get a couple of teeth drilled at the dentist. The doctor was this creepy old guy who always said, 'this won't hurt' and then it did. So the whole week leading up to the appointment, I was terrified."

"What happened?"

"I drank a whole bunch of vodka mixed with a bit of orange juice and I never felt a thing until I woke up in the middle of the night in the back seat of my mom's car."

"You passed out?"

"Completely. So I staggered into the house, starving, and found some old Chinese food."

"Uh-oh..."

"Yep. About ten minutes later I started losing all of that and more. I was so sick. I felt like shit for days. Between my initial traumatic experience and my general lack of resonance with alcohol, I never drank. I don't think I've missed anything."

The waitress returns and the Miracle orders another. I do a quick mental inventory and realize she has consumed two here and at least three glasses of wine at dinner, but hey, no biggie. This is a festive evening. For about an hour we engage in some pleasant conversation while she orders herself another round. She starts to slur her words a bit and jump between subjects. I guess it took me a while to notice that over the course of the evening, the Miracle has gotten rather intoxicated.

50

Since I am the one driving, this is of no great concern. I hand the waitress my card and pay the bill.

As we stand up to leave, the Miracle declares, "I think I want another one."

Did I detect an edge?

"Hey sweet pea, it's getting late. We've had a wonderful night, let's go home and make wild love."

"No, I'm getting another one," and with that she heads inside. Twenty minutes later she comes back with not only her drink, but also a handsome young man. Slightly slurring, "This is Michael. He was nice enough to buy me a drink, because you wouldn't."

The lad immediately realizes he has inadvertently stepped into the middle of something dissonant. The poor guy. What moments ago might have appeared to be a wandering beauty in search of drink (good), is obviously the partner of another dude (bad).

I reach out to shake his hand. "Michael, it's nice to meet you."

He reaches back awkwardly. "Actually, my name is Robert. Hey, nice meeting you both, but I'm going to go back inside with my fraternity brothers…"

She laughs. "Robert! I am so sorry. You reminded me of someone I know named Michael, this super cute guy at the mall who has a crush on me… and I kind of have a crush on him too… Oh, I can't say…." She turns to him and lowers her voice, but not so much that I can't still hear every word. "I have a boyfriend." She gestures my way. "But he doesn't want to buy me a drink. He's probably trying to save money. He doesn't even like to spend money on Christmas; it's really sad."

Uh-oh.

Our magical night is going straight into the toilet and there appears to be nothing I can do about it. What a bummer. The evening started out so happily, and then at some point we entered the Alcohol Twilight Zone.

Should I just leave her here with this young man? I'm sure she could, or more accurately would, end up with someone more than willing to put up with anything she does simply to look at her striking face. I feel numb and powerless. What can I do?

God, what time is it? 1:48 a.m.

This feels way beyond me at this point. I've got to go home.

The poor young guy sits there for a few more moments, probably wondering how he walked into this mess. She babbles on about a variety of unconnected subjects, augmented by an occasional wild outburst of laughter. I'm much too tired to be embarrassed for her. Then she abruptly decides she wants another one. "Which one of you two men wants to buy me my next round?"

"Not me." I blurt out. "In fact, I think I'm going to head home. Michael—I'm sorry, *Robert*—do you want to take her home, or somewhere, when she's done?"

The young guy catapults out of his seat. "Nice meeting you guys," he shouts over his shoulder as he quickly disappears inside.

I start toward the car. The Miracle stands up and almost falls over.

"Hey, wait for me; you can't just leave me here! Slow down, man."

"Do you think you can walk?" I'm more exhausted than angry.

"I'm fine. Lighten up. You just don't get it because you don't drink. I feel like you are trying to control me." A few steps behind me, she slowly staggers to the car.

On the short drive home there is nothing but silence until she says, "Do you hate me?"

"No. Let's just put this night to bed and talk in the morning when we are both clear."

"Oh, so you're not going to fuck me? I bet you will if I want you to." She smiles and puts her hand on the inside of my leg. "You know you can't say no, even if you're mad at me."

"I think tonight I'll pass."

She sags. "You do hate me. Well, we'll see what happens when we get into bed."

As we walk into the house, she says, "I'm going to sleep in the empty guest room. If you don't want me, I don't want you. In fact, I should have never come back here from California in the first place. It was the biggest mistake of my life."

She heads up the stairs. "You lost out, mister! We could have had quite the wild night if you weren't so controlling."

She slams the door.

Peter Pan pops his drowsy head out of his room and asks, "Hey, is everyone alright?"

"I'm sorry, brother, if we woke you up. I'll fill you in come morning."

"Are we still working on the book tomorrow?"

"Nothing can stop us now."

He manages a weary smile. "Good. Get some sleep, my friend."

Chapter 8

"Until we have seen someone's darknes
We don't really know who they are.
Until we have forgiven someone's darkness,
We don't really know what love is."
Marianne Williamson

I open the guest room door. She appears to be asleep with a pillow over her head and only a sheet covering a little of her leg. I whisper, "Are you alright?"

She groans. "Oh my God. I feel so sick. What time is it?"

"About three o'clock. It's a gorgeous day."

She peeks from behind the pillow then turns over. "So late?"

"Love, would you like a latte?"

"I would love one. Let me take a hot shower."

About twenty minutes later we are sitting across from each other in the living room. "Pauly, I need some aspirin. My head is pounding." She gets up and comes back. "This coffee is delicious. Thank you."

Where do I start and what do I say? "Any thoughts about last night?"

"I definitely should not have had so much to drink."

This makes me laugh. "An excellent insight."

"I'm sorry; I feel embarrassed. Do you hate me?" She looks down.

"I'm concerned. Do you think you need some help?"

"Help?"

I deliver the next line delicately. "Maybe a counselor, or a meeting... or something?"

"You mean like AA? I'm not an alcoholic. I just had too much to drink last night. It seems worse because you don't drink. Don't worry..."

"I feel concerned, I mean it's one thing..."

"Ah, Pauly... really, don't worry. I'm done drinking; that's it for me. Maybe just a glass of wine now and then, but right now even a glass feels like too much."

I take a sip out of a bottle of water. "Do you want to talk about the things you said?"

She puts her hand on her head; she obviously feels horrible. "I'm not sure I can even remember what I said, but whatever it was, I'm sorry. I was ripped." She gets up and sits next to me, puts my arm over her shoulder and leans into me. "I am so sorry. I love you, Pauly."

"Let me show you something." I pick up a perfect piece of paper and hand it to her. "Crumple it up. I mean, into a ball."

She takes it and squishes the paper into a round mass.

"OK. Now unfold it and make it smooth again. Make it as smooth as possible."

When she is done I take the paper from her and hold it up. "Look at this. Yes, it is fairly smooth, but you see all these lines and wrinkles? They will never go away.

"This piece of paper is our relationship, and these lines are the mean things we say to each other that we can never take back. Saying *I'm sorry* straightens the paper out, but it doesn't take away the wrinkles."

She frowns and looks away, takes a deep breath then looks back at me. "Not to make excuses, but I swear, a lot of it—if not all of it—is my job. I feel like it's changing me, making me unyielding and angry. There's something about the energy of the place that just drains me. I hate it, and my feet are always sore, even after a couple of days off. It's torture."

"I feel for you. Look, it's almost the end of April. Don't you get some kind of bonus in May?"

"May fifteenth, but I don't think I can make it."

"Three and a half weeks?"

She grimaces and shakes her head. "I doubt it, but I'll try. I have to quit or it will be the end of me."

"Can you just find some peace in knowing it's temporary? Why let it bother you when you know you're leaving?"

She pleads with me. "I'm telling you: my feet hurt all the time, I hate my boss, the mall has crummy energy, and all of it is sucking the life out of me."

I certainly can't argue. When she's not at the Church of Consumption, the Miracle is either pissed off or just wants to check out.

As much as I love her, I feel protective of my burgeoning book, perhaps in the same way as a mother with a newborn. The Miracle is obviously in distress but, with the project in the home stretch, I am bit nervous about her coming home full-time and messing up the editing dynamics. Is the job really that bad? Can't she just hang on for a few more weeks? I feel strongly pulled in both directions. Maybe I should let her quit. "Is the latte helping?"

"A lot. Pauly, I am so sorry."

I hug her. "I love you. It's so lovely out. Are you up for a sunset walk around the lake? Let's get outside and we can talk while we walk on the trails."

"Yes." She gives me a kiss. "Let me change."

A short seven-minute drive brings us to the local nature sanctuary.

With thirteen hundred acres of trails, wildlife and wonder that always lift my spirits, Radnor Lake is my favorite place in Nashville. We park by the Visitor's Center and walk up the hill where the beauty of the reservoir unfolds before us. About half way around the lake trail, we catch something rare and sublime: two bald eagles canvassing the water for fish.

"Look at the size of the those wings," I whisper in awe. "They are mystical creatures."

I hear the words of Chief Seattle in my heart: *All things are connected like the blood that unites us. Man did not weave the web of life, he is merely a strand in it...*

As we watch the pair circle, the Miracle says, "Pauly, those birds are us."

I lean in close to her. "Yes... and in terms of me, definitely the bald part."

She laughs and holds my arm. "No silly, two angels soaring, two of a kind, that's us."

I squeeze her hand. "I love you so much. Look at the light dancing on the water." We hear a stirring and catch a family of four deer making their way down to the edge of the lake for a drink. There are three adults and a very tiny fawn maybe ten yards in front of us.

"A baby..." She whispers. The deer browse about the vegetation and pick at a few leaves. A couple of bullfrogs near the water's edge have begun a steady dialog back and forth. A few fireflies can be seen dancing between the trees. The group of deer moves gingerly. They all appear so fragile and frail. I pause and say, "God, life is so miraculous."

She looks up and closes her eyes as if to soak it into her soul. "It is with you. Hey, I am so sorry about last night."

Looking at the deer, and then the eagles, I say, "Let's learn from it and let it go."

We walk for miles in silent awe, humble witnesses to nature's glory.

Later that evening, as we lay on top of our bed and a candle burns in our room, she confides, "I apologize for being so hard on you lately. I realize, in a way, I am not arguing with you, but with my father."

I turn to her beside me. "Why?"

"Growing up in a strict fundamental Christian home, the women are always treated as second-class citizens whose opinions don't matter. I saw my father treat my mother that way. In that world the man is always right. It's biblical. The woman and her feelings are almost meaningless."

"I'm sorry."

"No matter what I did, it was never good enough. I never measured up. That was only part of the insanity."

"Miracle, I remember you talking about this in Del Mar. You told me some of it but said it was too hard to go into."

"Well, here's something I've never shared with anyone. When I was young, we were forced to picket at abortion clinics and yell 'Murderer' at the people who came and went. I was just a little girl so it was quite horrifying. I had nightmares for years over this stuff."

I hold my arms around her tightly and just listen.

She breathes deeply. "I've been told my whole life what a wicked sinner I am and that I'm going to hell. After a while, I guess you start to believe it and act accordingly. I remember there were months when I was not permitted to leave the house for some imaginary transgression. We could never even have a non-Christian friend. It was all so depressing and confusing. Most of the time I didn't even want to be alive."

"My Lord, how did you cope?"

"I fought back, I gave up, I hid, I checked out, I smoked pot, I skipped school, but nothing worked. All of this madness still haunts me."

Not knowing what words I could say to ever heal such deep wounds, I hold her.

"I'm sorry," she says through tears. "I love you so much."

"Oh sweet girl, I regret you had to live through such pain. But don't worry. Everything is going to be all right. I love you more because you shared this. I need to do a better job of hearing you when you are trying to communicate difficult things to me like the stress of your job."

"Thank God I have you. You're my family and home. You're all I have."

As the candle flickers in the darkness, she dissolves into me, eventually falling asleep with her face pressed tightly against my tear-stained tee shirt.

Chapter 9

"The earth turned to bring us closer, it spun on itself and within us, and finally joined us together in this dream. Nights passed by, snowfalls and solstices; time passed in minutes and millennia. The earth was spinning with its music carrying us on board; it didn't stop turning a single moment as if so much love, so much that's miraculous was only an adagio written long ago in the Symposium's score."
Eugenio Montejo

The late morning sun is blasting through the large pane windows of the dining room as Peter Pan and I trade lines on the book with a bevy of notes and corrections culled from months of shaping this work.

The Miracle, dressed to the nines in full work attire, makes an unexpected entrance. "Hi, guys, how's it going?"

I get up and give her a hug. "Did you walk home from the mall? I thought you were working until six?"

She puts her bag on the table, gives a long exhale and sits down. "Well, I just got fired."

Peter Pan puts aside his pen. "Wow, what happened?"

She shakes her head. "I'm not sure. Our sales have broken records, the store looks sharp, but I just think my boss and I clashed. My guess is he wants to put his new boyfriend into my position."

I can't resist. "I am sure, among many other positions..."

The Miracle frowns. "Part of me is relieved, another part is in shock, and I also feel sad. I put so much into this job, and to be let go without any notice just hurts." Her eyes fill with tears. "I'm sorry. I didn't mean to cry."

I jump up and give her a hug. "Don't worry; besides, you were going to quit anyway. This was the universe's way of saying, 'enough is enough.' We will be fine." I rub her shoulders. "So get out of those crazy-ass shoes. Are you hungry? I could make you a smoothie."

The Miracle looks back at me. "I can't believe I got fired. I know I hated the job, but it still hurts."

Peter Pan shakes his head. "Of course it does. You had a lot invested." He looks at me and holds up some of the notes. "Hey, we've had a good day of work. You take care of her."

She perks up a bit. "Pauly, why don't we go grab a couple salads and then take a walk around the lake?"

I give her a hug. "There you go. Way to bounce back! You have been emancipated and your mall prison time commuted. Does this mean I don't have to rub your feet anymore?"

Peter Pan shakes his head. "He's just nuts..."

An hour later, the Miracle and I are slowly walking around the lake holding hands. The vegetation is lush, the birds singing, there are ducks on the water, and flowers bursting forth as the Nashville spring is in full bloom. The humidity is also starting to creep up. We linger along the path at a few clearings and soak up the sanctuary's visual blessings.

A long silence is broken by the Miracle's tender voice. "Pauly, is there something wrong with me?"

"Let me think about that... well... you could be a few inches taller."

She slaps my arm. "No, seriously, why can't I hold a job?"

I consider this as we meander along the pine-lined trail. "My feeling is: you are extremely sensitive, and while it is a gift on the human level, it does not lend itself well to the rigors of corporate life, or, God forbid, spending fifty hours a week at a small store in a mall. That type of environment is not conducive to the human spirit."

"Yes..."

"You are deeply empathetic."

She softly squeezes my hand. "I feel everything; that's why I tend to numb out. Sometimes it is just too overwhelming for me. But what should I do?"

I give the question some thought. "The first thing that pops into my head is how gifted you are at creating a beautiful home environment. Look what you have been able to do on a shoestring budget with our place. Not everyone can look at an empty room and turn it into something lovely."

"I enjoy decorating. Can you think of anything else?"

"I've been saying since we met that you would make an effective intuitive. Maybe you could guide people towards their own inner voice, and perhaps help them find their life's purpose. Look how much you have helped me. I count on your vision to see around the corners before we get there. Plus, you are adept with people. Maybe you should start a coaching/healing practice and see what happens."

"Do you think I could?"

"I know you can."

She leans in. "Hug and kiss me. I love you. You so believe in me."

"Hey the first line in my book says, 'I believe in Miracles.' And I do."

"Oh, Pauly, and I'm your Miracle?"

"You are."

Chapter 10

With a thousand ideas dancing in my head, I wake before the sunrise and grab my little journal. It's 4:44 a.m. Between thoughts I jot down a few notes. The Miracle lies blissfully sleeping in the next room. Why am I so awake? I decide to take a long meandering walk in the cool night air. As I move along the damp sidewalks, the giant oaks and the stars invite my reverence. Somewhere, a night bird's song fills the neighborhood with joyful melodies.

I walk for miles until the sun begins her slow entrance over the hills to the east. Returning, the house is still silent and my girl is still sleeping. Looking over the book notes I realize we are in the homestretch. The baby is getting close to birth.

A few hours later, Peter and I are in our familiar places at the table, tossing ideas back and forth when the Miracle returns from the gym. After grabbing something from the kitchen she comes into the room.

"Do you guys mind if I join you?"

Peter Pan looks quickly at me, since it is ultimately my call. I look back to him and he appears to be holding his breath.

There is only a second to decide, but it hangs there for what feels like an eternity.

Hey, maybe she just wants to see how we do this?

"Sure, why not." I gesture at an empty chair. "Have a seat and behold Peter's genius."

There is an obvious danger here because the chemistry has been so pitch perfect. After seven months of daily work a tremendous amount of trust has been created between the two of us. This has given birth to a beautiful, yet fragile creative intimacy. Besides, I'm not sure that editing a book is designed to be a spectator sport.

Peter Pan and I begin bantering an idea back and forth for a couple of minutes when the Miracle suddenly breaks in.

"You guys are still dawdling on these minor details after all of these months? You need to get down to it." She hits the table. "I mean, some of these issues should have been addressed the first time you went through the thing."

She points at Peter Pan. "You are too nice to him. Don't coddle him or his feelings. Just be honest; it's the only way this thing is going to get done or be any damned good."

Peter P begins to mount a defense. "You can't jump all over the talent or you will shut down his creativity. It's like when I produced records: you never got on the singer, because he or she would close off and tighten up. The artist has to feel safe..."

She interrupts PP. "May I look?" He hands over the pages and she reads a few lines. "I mean, some of this is good, but it still needs a lot of work."

My mouth hangs open. If I had a boxing ring bell, I would ring it. "Hey, we need a time-out. This intrusion is highly destructive to our process."

Peter Pan says, "Maybe I should go."

This is a seminal moment for me and for her. It's one thing to argue about drinking, or how messy she is, even money, but this is my work, my baby and no one fucks with it. There is nothing wrong with conscious, well-delivered feedback, but this seems like abstract frustration masquerading as 'being helpful,' and I'll have none of it.

I stand up. "Peter, you sit tight." I look at her. "Can we take a moment in the other room one-on-one?"

"Sure." She tosses the pages on the table and goes on ahead of me.

I turn back to PP. "I'll be right back."

"Man, I'm sorry, but you can't let her mess with your art. That would be tragic. Hang tough..."

In our room, we sit on the bed. "Girlfriend, what was that all about? You came in on us guns a-blazing."

"Pauly, you have been editing for months, and it's not even close. Someone needs to get real here and bring this thing to completion. I was only trying to help."

"I know your intentions were good, but your execution was, well, more like an execution. No finesse. No sensitivity. That won't work, and it will only obfuscate whatever point you hoped to share."

"Pauly, I just want to help. Remember I have had some good insights too."

I put my arm around her shoulder. "You have definitely made some positive suggestions, lots of them and they have been incorporated. Look, I'm glad you no longer have your dreadful job hanging over your head, but we have been at this for close to seven months and have established a method to our madness. You have to leave us to it and trust it will be done well. Believe me when I say we can see the finish line."

She looks shocked. "Wait. Are you choosing him over me?"

"Not as a boyfriend, no."

"Don't joke with me. Is that what you are doing?"

"I'm continuing to work with him on my book. The key phrase being 'my book.' You are my life partner, not my literary collaborator. In fact, I think it's healthy to keep some things separate. What if I had come down to your store and started telling you everything you had created there was wrong and suggested radical changes? You would kick my sorry ass out."

"Are you kicking me out?"

"Only out of the editing process, not the house. But don't push it." I laugh, but she misses the joke.

She suddenly looks deeply sad.

"Can I borrow the car?"

"Of course. Where are you going?"

"I have no idea. Maybe shopping."

"Funny."

A moment later the door slams and she is gone.

I come back in and Peter Pan gives me a weary look. "Everything okay?"

"Am I nuts?"

"Yes, but that's an entirely different discussion."

I laugh, which is a godsend. "She isn't too happy about it, but what else could I do? It was like a bull in a china shop. A bull wearing cute boots, but a bull nonetheless."

Peter Pan exhales. "We almost had a Yoko-in-the-studio situation, but thankfully you headed it off at the pass."

"Why do I feel I may end up with a book, but lose the girl?"

He picks up the pages she tossed and reorganizes them a bit.

"There is a chance that might happen. But you can't sell your art out, and trust me when I say you have something special here. I know I never praise you, because honestly you just don't need it. You have such a freaking gift. I have no idea how you do it, but you do."

"Thank you… but man I don't…"

He is standing and holding up the manuscript. "I have a feeling people are going to respond to this. Even though I am not the *cosmic* one at the table, I think there is a destiny here. This is your job, this is your calling, and I'm here to be the cynical guy, to keep it real, and this shit is *real*. So don't let anyone tell you differently—even if they have a dazzling face and you love them madly—this work matters." He raises his voice and lifts the papers. "This is really good shit."

I'm stunned for a moment. I've never seen him riled up. "I had no idea you felt this way."

He eyes widen. "Are you kidding? Do you know how much time I've put into this thing?" He augments his voice. "Countless hours, but I love it like you do. I think about it all the time, and I look forward to our morning hours batting the muse around. This has been a light for me during a very dark time. It has given me something to feel good about. I needed this, and you needed me."

"I did… more than you know…"

"We both did, and it's been a blessing." He sits back down. "So let's wrap this baby up and get it out there in the world where someone, somewhere might smile or get an insight into this crazy fucking world. Or just have a good laugh, or a moment's reprise."

"Wait a second."

His eyes widen, "Oh shit, now what?"

"Do you think we should burn some sage?"

Chapter 11

"Art is never finished, only abandoned."
Leonardo da Vinci

One month later to the day, on a warm afternoon while hiking the high trail, I cast my cares out across Radnor Lake. I have been coming here alone more often these days just to get some time to clear my head. A couple of meandering miles down the path, I come upon a bald eagle sitting majestically just a few feet above me in a pine tree.

I slowly sit down.

How long will he tolerate my presence?

He looks upon me briefly, and then returns his gaze across the placid water. I study the impeccable structure of his form, the beauty of his feathers, and the strength of his talons.

He appears at peace up there in the tree.

He suddenly stirs and there is a rush of sound as he unfolds his massive wings, stopping briefly, and then takes flight. A breeze rushes over me and I spontaneously gasp at his high-end aerodynamic abilities.

His presence is humbling enough, but to see him unfurl and defy gravity is truly a wordless privilege.

As I watch him soar across the water and then out of my line of sight, I feel a strong sense that my memoir is complete.

The wind whispers to me...

Tie a ribbon around your work and release her on golden wings to the waiting world.

Through some good old-fashioned detective work, I manage to finagle someone into putting a copy in his hands.

A couple of weeks later one sunlit day in May, Peter Pan asks, "Do you think you will ever hear anything from Larry?"

"Truthfully? No." We both laugh. "But I didn't want to surprise him. We will never know if he even sees it. But this way, if I ever run into him again, I can honestly say I sent it his way first."

Peter P endorses my choice. "That's good life business. Man, I have to tell you. I miss the morning sessions and our work together. There's such a void now."

"You and me both. It feels odd to stop the process, but I guess at some point you have to say enough."

That evening I sit at a small salon and watch as the Miracle gets her rock star locks trimmed. I can't curb my enthusiasm, "Look at your hair! You should seriously consider modeling, or at least doing hair advertisements."

Her stylist, Very Gay Todd, poured ever so tightly into his black leather pants, adds, "Sweetheart, you should definitely get some pictures taken. I think you are the most striking woman to ever sit in this chair."

She blushes. "You guys are pumping me up." As stunning as she is, a part of her has always been shy about her looks. She often tells me, "It is both a blessing and curse."

I point to my head. "Todd, can you do anything for me?"

He laughs. "Need a trim do you? I think the Bruce Willis look works for you. It's very rugged, and you do have a wonderfully shaped head."

"It's just that my head is two sizes too large."

He smiles. "Tough to buy a hat?"

"Funny, I once went into a place in Key West to buy a hat and the guy wanted to measure the inseam of my pants."

They both laugh.

"Oh my Pauly," the Miracle says. "Don't mind him."

Very Gay Todd raises an eyebrow. "Is this rascal always like this?"

She laughs. "Usually much worse..."

My phone pings, so I take a look. It's an e-mail:

Paul,

Imagine my surprise when your book showed up. I can't believe you have created this; what a wonderful piece of work!

Of course, if I had only known, I would have been wittier.

It is very well done.

All the best and good luck,

Larry David

PS: I hope I see you again along the South Road

I take a moment to try to process it... I don't succeed, so read I it again. Then I check the e-mail name. Then I reread the email... then...

HOLY SHIT! LARRY DAVID READ THE BOOK! LARRY READ THE BOOK!

A startled Very Gay Todd turns playfully to the Miracle and says, "Holy shit. But who the hell is Larry David?"

Of course the Miracle knows. "Oh, Pauly, that is tremendous. You are a magician. I told you he would read it. What did he say?"

I read her the e-mail, and then she makes me do it again. Her hands over her mouth, her eyes wide, she says, "I am so happy for you."

"Be happy for us. This is our adventure, our book, our life, and it is so much better sharing it with you." I give her a kiss on the forehead.

Very Gay Todd chimes in, "Listen to Romeo here. He certainly sounds like a writer. Will somebody please tell me who the hell this Larry David character happens to be? Is that the chubby dude who plays the cable guy?"

The Miracle interjects, "He created *Seinfeld*, and is on the show *Curb Your Enthusiasm*."

"Oh, the bald fella who has all the quirks. He's funny and kind of cute in a crazy neurotic type of way. Definitely not my type; I like brawn, not brains."

The Miracle is beaming. "Pauly! We have to celebrate."

I look at her in all her glory. "We also need to celebrate your hair. My lord. I'm speechless. Todd, you are an artist."

He shrugs. "Are you kidding? It's easy when you have someone so magnificent as this creature here. And darling, you are such a sweetie pie. We need to go grab a drink sometime and have girl talk."

Chapter 12

"Once you make a decision
The universe conspires to make it happen"
Ralph Waldo Emerson

With the temperatures rising here in Nashville, my daydreams take me back to the cool New England breezes of Martha's Vineyard.

One fine early June morning over granola, the Miracle asks, "Pauly what should we do this summer?"

"Funny, I was just thinking about Martha's Vineyard. It sure would be wonderful to go back."

"Can we swing it?"

"I'm not sure how to make it work. To rent anything is prohibitively expensive. We could probably stay at the Asylum for about a week, but not much more."

"It's the same for me with my parents. Remember though, your dad did invite us to come visit. When will the book be ready?"

"Hopefully, they'll be in print by the end of the month. I guess we could always try to sell a few copies and use the money we make for rent. Even if we break even, we would be way ahead."

She crinkles up her nose for a moment, then rolls her tongue around in her mouth, fiddles with her hair, and looks up at me. "I'm game."

I raise my finger. "I have an idea. Maybe we could stay with Larry."

She laughs. "Send him an e-mail. You guys seem to have a cool thing between you. Then your sequel could be called *Living With Larry David.*"

"It has a ring to it. I can see it as a part of a never-ending series. *Camping With Larry David*, and so on."

Her soft hand takes mine. "But seriously, I'd love to see the Vineyard again. It's such a heavenly place, and those two weeks we spent there last summer were just too short. I think being there together would once again be healing."

Sometimes our wishes go unheard, and sometimes they are granted in the most unusual ways.

The next day I get a call from an unfamiliar number in New York City. "Hey cowboy, how would you like to be a caretaker in paradise?"

"I'm sorry. Who is this?"

"Wait. You don't know? Then fuck you."

"Come on. At least give me a hint. Is this a time-share pitch?"

"Time-share? Okay, asshole. Last summer I picked you up hitchhiking and you ended up coming to my house in Chilmark for lobster dinner. You played the piano and I even offered you my place for the winter. But you turned your nose up at it like a finicky cat. You spoiled piece of shit. I can't believe you already forgot me."

It takes me a moment, but somewhere my inner Google turns up a short bald man with a handlebar mustache and sour disposition. "Jack Daniels! The little prick himself. How the hell are you?" (I never ever talk to anyone like this, but believe it or not, this is Jack's preferred method of communication. Go figure.)

"Ok, so now you remember. Hey, I don't have time for small talk with a tiny nobody like you while the stock market is open. I was calling to see if you wanted to be my caretaker this summer."

"You are beyond care. Remember, I am not a licensed psychotherapist, you douche bag."

76

"There you go... but not me, ass wipe. My crib. The house..."

"Just for kicks, besides putting up with you, which sucks, what does this gig entail?

"You would basically watch other people work. We have gardeners, maids, a pool guy, landscapers, window washers, and whatever else you can think of. You name it. We got it. I want you to watch over all of them and keep them honest. For some crazy reason I trust you."

"Well, we all know you are a misguided cantankerous fuck. I don't recall anything there worth stealing. Honestly, I'm not sure I could stand to see you more than in passing... and even then only from a distance..."

"You're right. But better yet, you won't even have to put up much with me. We only fly up in my plane on the weekends. Obviously the house is big enough for a mob, but if you want to get lost while we're there, I won't mind."

My mind drifts back to a tremendous home with large windows everywhere overlooking the western shoreline, with a custom pool and sprawling acres of well-manicured grounds. I remember the wife was nice in an uptight kind of way. What else? Oh yeah, this guy drank a ton of whiskey and had an edge to him. It could be risky.

"By the way, assuming I was foolish enough to accept this terrible offer, when would you need me?"

"Yesterday. When can you get here?"

I think for a few seconds about the logistics of it all. "Probably within a week. Let me check with my girlfriend and see what she thinks."

"Wait... girlfriend? When did you con someone into being your squeeze? Is this one of those mail-order

brides from Russia? Is she hot? I hope so. We can't
have any more ugly women around the house; it's
enough my wife lives there. What a ball buster. I'd
divorce her, but she would take everything, even the
Swiss bank accounts."

He makes me laugh. "I remember you guys were
like Romeo and Juliet with sharp knives."

"Ha, ha..."

These two hated each other... but a free mansion
in the Vineyard for the summer would be a godsend
with the book coming out. Why not?

"Can I call you at this number tomorrow and let
you know?"

"Of course. Oh, and fuck you." And Jack Daniels
hangs up.

I track down the Miracle and bounce the idea off of
her. "What do you think of house-sitting in the Vineyard
for the summer in a palatial mansion overlooking the
ocean?"

"Really?"

"Scout's honor."

"Did you ask Larry to watch his house?"

I smile. "I did not. But it's a real offer."

"What's the catch?"

"We have to put up with a guy who's a jerk and
drinks a shitload of whiskey. But the good news is, he
and his wife only fly over on the weekends and we can
leave when they're there."

"Where would we go?"

"Somewhere into the woods."

She laughs. "Seriously..."

I consider her question. "Maybe we could stay
with my parents a few nights and then improvise a
bit? I have a lot of friends there plus maybe we could
luck into a rental. A few nights with the parents..."

"Would your mom and dad let us?"

"I could ask."

"It sounds wonderful. When do they want us?"

"Right away!"

It doesn't take her long to think about it. "Why not? Let's go. We can always come home."

I dial my parents up in Martha's Vineyard, and my Dad picks up.

"Dad, we have an opportunity to house-sit up in Chilmark for the summer. The place is huge and we would have it during the week to ourselves, but may need a place on certain weekends to find refuge from some crazy folks."

"The owners?" Dad was always so street smart.

"You got it."

"Well, why don't you stay at the cabin on weekends, and with them during the week. It would be a treat to see you. When are you coming?"

"Probably in a week." I hold my breath a bit because I'm not really sure how he will react. Yes, he invited us to come see them. But maybe when confronted with us actually coming, he will change his mind.

There is a short silence. "I'll let your mother know. She'll be excited to see you. Hopefully we will all be together soon."

Exhale. "Thanks Dad. I love you and Mom."

"We love you too. Talk soon..."

Chapter 13

Synchronicity:
The simultaneous occurrence of events
That appears to be significantly related
But have no discernible causal connection

Five days later we drive our Prius onto the ferry in Woods Hole for the delicious 45-minute trek across to paradise.

With its New England charm and captivating beauty, the Vineyard sits nobly off the base of Cape Cod a mere seven miles from what most of us consider reality. With her pristine beaches and endless miles of green space, the Island feels like heaven. There are no traffic lights, billboards, highways, or malls on this rock. An unguarded feeling permeates people's attitudes and tends to relax their faces. Yes I know, it sounds almost un-American, but this is precisely the charm of the place.

After a phenomenal night's sleep in the Parental Asylum, we awaken on our first Vineyard day to an endless blue sky and a slight chill in the air. Spooning the Miracle on a crisp morning is certainly one of life's sweetest pleasures. Her soft skin, the feel of her body, and the most fragrant natural scent ever make it hard to get out of bed.

The air is cold, but my parents' smiles are warm, welcoming and joyful. My mom gives me the longest hug. "Good morning. I love you, darling. My baby is home and all grown up." Dad embraces everyone and shares small talk. Heck, even Max is all fired up and out in his fenced pen, chasing after imaginary pestilence.

After goodbyes, we grab a couple of mandatory cappuccinos down in the heart of Edgartown, before heading off to Chilmark to check in as caretakers. Having house-sat before, I am relaxed. But the Miracle is a bit tense.

"So we will live in these people's house?"

"Yes."

"Will they be there?"

"Some of the time. But I think when they come back, we should go someplace else."

She bites her lower lip and furrows her brow. "I don't know about this. Are you sure it's a good idea?"

"Well, it's all we have right now if we want to stay on the Island. As welcoming as my folks were, we can't stay at the Parental Asylum for more than a couple of scattered nights. That would be too risky. Besides, think of it as adventure. Or even better, like owning a mansion with none of the worries."

She gives me one of her patented 'I don't think so' looks.

We arrive at a palatial estate with panoramic views in all directions.

"Is this it?" She gasps. "This place is expansive. Look Pauly, there is a pool, and those gardens... You can see the ocean and hear the waves. Oh my God..."

But before we are even out of the car, Jack Daniels is running towards us and looking over his shoulder. "Hey you guys." He looks back again.

"Is someone chasing you with a knife?"

"Worse. I just told the Evil Queen about our wonderful new summer caretakers and she was none too pleased. By the way, and holy cow, who is this goddess?"

I gesture towards the insane little man. "Miracle, I would like you to meet Jack Daniels."

JD points towards her. "OK, so you feel sorry for him, right?" He's crouching as if trying to avoid a sniper's bullet.

The Miracle smiles, "I do feel very sorry him."

I pipe in, "Actually she's raised me since I was a pup. But wait a minute. You just told your wife about us today? Jack, are you nuts?"

"Is that a rhetorical question? Look, I'm hoping my wife will get used to the idea. Come on in. I'll introduce you guys."

The Miracle gives me another of those patented 'I told you so' looks as we venture cautiously towards the front door.

Once inside, a short, fit woman of about 60 greets us with the worst shit-eating-fake-smile I have ever seen.

It doesn't take me long to realize we are just collateral damage in their long running war. She is obviously furious with Jack Daniels, but is attempting to pull this off in a civil fashion. Then, after we depart, she can kill asshole Jack and throw his body out in the compost pile, where it belongs.

After a few minutes tour of the place and awkward small talk discussing a few of our rather limited 'responsibilities,' the Evil Queen departs. It's quickly decided amongst the three of us that the new caretakers should likewise beat a hasty retreat.

Jack Daniels walks us to the car while constantly looking back towards the house, as if he feared something very sharp might suddenly fly in his direction.

"Why don't you come back tomorrow evening after we fly out of here and make yourself at home. I'll call you this week if we need anything. Just enjoy the place and give it time; she will get used to you guys.

I nod. "If you insist."

Jack shakes my hand. "Hopefully, I can come back a few times this summer without you-know-who and hang out with you guys. Wouldn't that be fun?"

Now it's my turn to present the same fake smile the Evil Queen had on her face. "Ah yes, of course. That would be a, well, a blast."

As we make our way back down the long and winding driveway, the Miracle says, "Oh Pauly."

I quickly shift into recovery mode. "Was that a gorgeous house or what? The grass looked like a golf course and there is a hot tub with a view of the sea. They even have a garden with fresh veggies..."

Silence.

"Man, we are going to have so much fun in there. Did you see the view from our bedroom suite? Do you have any idea what that would cost if it was a fine hotel?"

Silence.

"OK, I'm sorry. Remember, it's only temporary." I think for a moment about the Evil Queen's reaction. "It might be very temporary. As in that ten minutes was the extent of our career in caretaking."

She chuckles. "Oh, Pauly."

"Hey, let's hit the Chilmark Store and celebrate with a slice of pizza. That should take the sting out of our impending termination."

The Miracle gives me a kiss on the cheek and says, "Lunch sounds good. Man, I can't get the wife's strange smile out of my head."

"Well, she had more teeth than the Osmond family."

She laughs. "Be nice, Pauly."

84

We pull in and walk up on the porch. I notice two open rockers in the corner. "Sweet Pea, why don't you grab those seats, and I'll go in and place an order for us?"

She has a very funny look on her face.

"Sweet Pea...what is it?"

She touches my arm. "You will never guess who is walking up right towards us."

I turn slowly and laugh out loud. "Well... of course... How crazy?"

Suddenly, he is upon us in all his glory. He shakes his head and says, "Oh my God, is that really you?"

"Indeed it is." We shake hands.

He's smiling. "When did you get here?"

"Last night."

"Me too. So this is your first full day?"

"Yes. Man, it's good to see you."

He pauses and ponders all of this for a moment, then smiles. "So I guess our thing from last year has carried over to this summer."

"It appears it has."

Then he does a serious, comedic double take. "Wait a minute, who is this fabulous woman? Is she with you? Are you with him?"

The Miracle smiles, "I am."

I concur. "She is..."

He appears to consider this, and then it clearly hits him. "Wait, is this the girl from the book? Is this... is this the Miracle?"

"It is. So you did read it?"

"Of course I read the book. I still can't believe you wrote... wait, but this girl is absolutely dazzling. How did you get a woman this lovely to date you?"

I put my finger up to my lips as if to say shhhhh, pass my hand in front of her face a couple of times, then mouth the words, "She's blind."

He cracks up. "You guys made it. How terrific. And you just got here today? Today?"

"We did. By the way let me introduce you both: Miracle, I would like you to meet Mr. Larry David."

Chapter 14

"If I had only known, I would have been wittier."
Larry David

The Miracle and I grab our lunches and take a couple of seats at the far end of the porch.

She leans in and whispers, "Larry is nice. It's obvious you two have a certain cosmic chemistry."

I shake my head. "How strange for us to run into each other on our first day back." I give it some thought. "Well, maybe not so strange."

Larry comes out with his lunch, looks down at us, and comes over. "Do you two mind if I join you?"

The Miracle smiles. "Of course not."

I open my arms in a welcoming motion. "Larry, this is the lunch we tried to have last summer."

He smiles. "The lunch we tried to have?"

I raise my hands. "Good point. The lunch I tried to have. Either way…"

The Miracle shakes her head. "You guys are funny."

Larry begins making a bit of a mess. "Do you happen to have an extra napkin?" She hands him a couple of hers. He surveys the scene. "But now you don't have any left."

"I'm not as sloppy as you."

He gives me the classic Larry David nod, and then points at me. "I have to say… I am impressed you could get a girl like this. It takes you to a whole new level." He turns to her, "So do you go hitchhiking with this guy?"

She laughs. "Not yet. But he has promised to take me at least once. He has a car now."

He seems a bit surprised. "You do?"

I point to the red Prius in the parking lot. "She's right there."

"A Prius? Good for you, I have one back in Los Angeles."

"I bought it to be more like you."

The Miracle slaps my arm. "No, he didn't; he had the Prius before you met."

He smiles. "She keeps you honest. A girl, a car...this is impressive. So, how long are you two planning to stay here?"

She and I look at each other, and she answers, "Hopefully for the summer, but we are house-sitting for some people who might be challenging." She laughs.

I jump in. "Larry, the people are nuts, but the house is luxurious. By the way, thank you for giving me the thumbs up on the book."

"I couldn't believe it when you sent it to me." He turns to her. "What do you think of the book?"

She beams. "I think it's amazing. We want to put it out this summer."

Larry puts down his salad and wipes his face. "I still can't believe you wrote that. How did you remember every detail?"

She answers for me. "He remembers everything. It's strange and creepy."

He chuckles. "Still, to write a book is impressive. Good luck with it. Has your dad read it?"

"Not yet." I say.

He gets a funny look in his eye. "That could be interesting. How are your parents anyway?"

I knock on wood. "Healthy, thank God."

"Well I hate to bring this up..." Larry looks like he is trying to choose just the right words. "But did you happen to honor our deal?"

I point at him. "Apparently I am not the only one with a good memory. You are speaking, of course, of my Faustian bargain to watch some of your stuff in exchange for the ride?"

He nods. "I am."

The Miracle laughs out loud at our comedic dance. "Go ahead and tell him."

Larry looks at her. "Remember, it's up to you to keep him honest."

I raise one hand. "I swear to tell the whole truth and nothing but the truth. We watched every single episode of *Curb Your Enthusiasm*. Every one! So our covenant is complete."

He turns again to her and gestures towards me. "Is he telling the truth?"

She smiles and laughs. "Yes, we loved them!"

I jump in. "They truly were terrific. Particularly the one with Wheelchair Wendy."

"You liked Wheelchair Wendy? Well then..." He reaches over and shakes my hand. "How about *Seinfeld*."

He has me on my heels a bit. "Not yet, but if you recall, I was allowed to pick one of the two."

He looks at me suspiciously. "True. So you still have never seen a single episode of *Seinfeld*?"

"Remember, I am not a TV guy."

The Miracle supports this claim. "He never watches television. I have to make him watch movies with me on DVD."

"But to never see *Seinfeld* is just off." He is having some fun.

"Here's an idea: what if we do something else, like play a round of golf. I would then be obligated to watch more shows."

Larry looks up and then at us. "My initial reaction is absolutely not."

The Miracle laughs out loud.

We spend the next thirty minutes making small talk about the Vineyard, certain beaches, the best places to eat, relationships, LA, and other odds and ends. Eventually he stands and says, "Well, I have to go. Thank you both very much." He turns to me and, with a glimmer in his eye, says, "I'm sure I will see you again."

We both smile and shake hands. He turns to the Miracle. "And it was a joy meeting you. I think people are going to like him a lot better with you around."

"Ah, thank you." She says.

Larry puts his hand on my shoulder. "By the way, I appreciate your portraying me so kindly in the book."

"I was only being honest. There is an ancient proverb: 'Never bite the hand... that picks you up hitchhiking.' Right?"

He smiles. "Regardless, you were very kind."

Larry departs and then returns a moment later with a handful of napkins. "You see, when you loan me napkins, you get more back in return. You never want to owe someone a bunch of napkins. I don't want this hanging over my head all summer..."

She and I laugh, because frankly, the whole thing is hysterical. As Larry walks away, he turns back and waves before disappearing over the horizon.

I turn to the Miracle. "Well, the summer is certainly off to an interesting start."

She gives me a kiss on the cheek. "Life is just an adventure with you."

"Miracle, why don't we walk off this pizza along the cliffs of Aquinnah?"

~~~

Aquinnah Flashback~

We spend our afternoons hanging out on the beach in Aquinnah, taking long walks past multi-colored cliffs hundreds of feet high. The cliffs, long ago etched over time by six glaciers, remain a holy place for the Island's original inhabitants, the Wampanoag Indian Tribe.

The Miracle and I take moist clay and cover our selves from head to toe. The sun dries the clay, creating a full body mask, removing toxins from our skin and hearts. Encased, we swim in a deserted cove as the water washes our souls clean.

This hallowed native ground blesses and heals us.

As the sun drifts into the sea, I realize I finally have found someone who will watch the sunset with me. With an old wool blanket wrapped around us, we observe the afterglow fill the sky. We sit with our mouths agape, marveling at the brilliance of the changing colors.

~~~

After parking the car and hiking down the path to the shore, we stroll along the beach at a leisurely pace. The sun is bright, the humidity low and the temperature is in the perfection zone. I turn to her. "Remember last summer, with only the ocean as a witness, you and I made love over there?"

She squeezes my hand. "Yes, as the sun was setting..."

"Years ago, I experienced my first profound spiritual experiences on these very sands. This stretch of coastline feels like my church."

The Miracle is randomly picking up shells as we chat. "Pauly, my family wants me to come back in late July for a family reunion. Part of me would love to see

91

them, but I am also leery of the whole dynamic. When together, we always fall into a pattern of negativity, and it drags me down."

I pick up a stone and skip it off the water. "That invite sort of came out of nowhere. How long would you be gone?"

"My mom sent me an email this morning. The whole thing would last about ten days; maybe two weeks. Wait, don't you want to come with me?" She laughs when she says it, but I know she is partially serious.

"I thought they didn't want to meet a heathen like me because of my belief systems. It would also be hard to leave all this." I slowly move my hand across the phenomenal vista, "But you know they might be better behaved with an outside observer lurking about. Would you like me to go for moral support?"

"I would love for you to come, but I'm not sure you would be welcome. They are not happy about us living in sin. It's the fundamentalist Christian thing rearing its head again. Remember, you haven't been saved."

"I was saved... that time I almost drown off South Beach."

"Pauly."

I smile and take her arm. "Speaking of sin, why don't we make love behind those dunes?"

She smiles. "Maybe..."

I put my arm around her shoulder. "You don't have to go back to your parents. You could politely decline and stay here in paradise. Or I can go with you."

She dips her feet in the water. "Oh my God, it's freezing. Come see..."

A wave wraps its arms around my feet. "Holy...!!! God that's cold... After growing up in

Florida with the surf in the eighties, I've never gotten used to these New England water temps."

She picks up a colorful shell. "This is lovely. Speaking of parents, yours seem genuinely glad to see us. What a shift from last year."

I look her in the eye. "Indeed. I pray things stay on the bright side. I can tell my dad is trying, which means a lot." I reach down and pick up a smooth beige stone. "Hey, let's make an offering to the Island gods with the hope that all this good energy holds up."

She laughs and hands me a small piece of driftwood. We toss both of them out to sea. "Pauly, I love it here. You know, this would be a sensational place for our wedding."

I point to a spot near the cliffs. "We could do it right there on the beach in our bare feet. Just you, me, God, and the seagulls."

She shakes her head. "Oh no, I don't want one of those hippie weddings with all kinds of weird rituals."

"No shaman and magical fairy dust? Are we going the traditional route then?"

She pauses, "Nothing too big or stiff like I had with my first wedding. Funny, I knew I was making a huge mistake, but I still went through with it."

"Remember, you were young, and you were playing a role."

She looks heavenward. "I was only twenty-four. God, I was a baby. What was I thinking?"

I lean over and kiss her. "I love you. Who thinks at that age? No one, really. It takes a while to figure things out. I barely know anything now. Thankfully, I have you to tell me what to do."

She grabs my waist and squeezes. "And don't you forget it, mister."

We wander the beach for a couple more hours, take a nap in the sand, and then, while holding hands, watch the sky fill with a kaleidoscope of colors.

Afterward, we take the long, scenic drive back to the cabin.

My mother greets us warmly. "Hello, you two lovely people. Did you have a nice day?"

The Miracle gives her a hug. "We did, and we even ran into Larry David."

My dad looks over and laughs. "Again? This is getting spooky. Did he mention the book?"

"He told Pauly he loves it. Larry joined us for lunch and we all had a wonderful time."

Dad shakes his head. "Well, you finally had the lunch you were joking about. What a wild story. And it just keeps going."

I give my dad a hug. "By the way, he specifically asked if you had read my book."

Miracle says, "He had a twinkle in his eye and he did inquire about you reading it."

My dad smiles. "Tell Larry I will in due time."

I pick up one of the copies. "Well, maybe it's better if you don't. I would hate for you to disinherit me."

He smiles. "It's too late, son. We're leaving everything here to the Veteran's Home."

I look around at the cabin's contents. "Do you think they'll take it?"

Mom laughs and the Miracle says, "Pauly!"

Mom shakes her head. "He's joking. It's so nice to have you both here. Did you have a good day?"

I give Mom a long hug. "We had an excellent day, and we even saw Larry David."

She looks surprised. "You did? How wonderful. I love you, darling. You will always be my baby boy."

Chapter 15

"Heaven is not a place, and it is not a time.
Heaven is being perfect.
Overcome space, and all we have left is Here.
Overcome time, and all we have left is Now."
Jonathan Livingston Seagull

The following weekend I get a call from our overlord. "Hey, Hitchhiker, I know it's Saturday and my ball-busting wife is here, but I would love it if you two would come up to the house for the sunset and a fabulous dinner."

I have to smile at Jack Daniels, because at least he tries. "Are you sure? Usually we stay in the lowlands when you and the Evil Queen are lurking about."

"You have to come; she's driving me nuts. I also have a surprise for you—and it's not the sight of me naked, so don't get too excited."

"Can we bring anything?"

"Just a good attitude. See you around six."

A few hours later we arrive and take a short stroll on the grass behind the house. I take off my sandals to feel the soft ground beneath my feet.

Jack finds us looking out at the sea. "Look at that sky!" He shakes my hand and gives her a peck on the cheek. "What a vista. It almost makes all the shit I have to put up with worth it."

We laugh.

"Hitchhiking Man, have I got a surprise for you. Actually, it's more of a gift." He's practically dancing on the grass, an ever-present evening drink in hand.

Jack Daniels Trivia: *Every evening when the clock chimes 5:00 p.m. (and not a moment after) Jack will pour himself a very tall glass of straight whiskey over ice. And then another... and then...*

By 7:00 pm he shifts into a kinder, gentler version of himself. By 9:00, he's ready to buy you whatever you want (iPad, a car, a boat, a home, whatever). By 11:00, he's usually conked out on the sofa.

He awakens in the morning, his usual tight-fisted asshole self. (I promised I would buy you what? No way...)

It is what is.

Jack Daniels gazes out at the water, then back at us. "Tonight, my dear friend Livingston Taylor is coming over for dinner and will probably play music." His eyes have a glint in them. "You know who Livingston Taylor is right?"

I smile and remember the first time I met Mr. Taylor.

~~~

Livingston Taylor Flashback~

One morning during the embryonic days of my hitchhiking career, I stick out my thumb and end up in Aquinnah. After a glorious day on the beach, I walk up to the road to catch a ride home. Within a minute, a truck pulls over and the driver sticks out his hand.

"Hi, I'm Livingston Taylor. Hop in."

We quickly fall into an interesting conversation regarding the nature of happiness, and Livingston shares his passion for flying. "There's nothing like being up in the air. Hey, do you have any time to come by my house and help me move some stuff?"

"Sure."

We end up at a seaside cabin that is more camp than palace. Stopping in front of a huge pile of junk, he says, "I'd like to move this outside."

96

"Sure."

"Wait a minute. The hell with this crap. I say we go flying."

I can't say yes fast enough.

We pull into the airport and board his single-engine Cessna. Within moments, we're up in the air and circling Fantasy Island. As the sun begins her blinding exit to the west, Livingston says, "Hey co-pilot, do you want to take over?"

Speechless, I seize the controls. Soon, like the seabirds I envy, I am flying. From my imperial vantage point, the array of colors and expansive views take on an impressionistic quality.

"Livingston, it feels like heaven up here."

"Yes. We are free."

"How did I ever get so lucky?"

"We both are, my friend." Though strangers in form, we are brothers in flight.

With time enforcing its inevitability, and the encroaching darkness insisting our adventure come to an end, we reluctantly become Earth-bound creatures once again.

~~~

An hour later, we're seated, along with a dozen others, around a large wooden table set to eat a buffet of fresh seafood. Though the Evil Queen appears none too pleased, Jack Daniels and the guests are enjoying themselves.

Sweet Livingston shares a few fabulous stories and observations.

After dinner he and I catch each other in the hall coming and going. "Livingston, you gave me a thrill one bright day a while ago when you took me flying."

He laughs and says, "I did?"

"Yes. You picked me up hitchhiking and an hour later we were circling the island in your Cessna."

Liv seems to search his memory then shakes his head. "I honestly have no memory of it, but I'm sure it happened. There was an extended period of my life when I was having way too much fun. Some things have completely slipped through the cracks. Please tell me I was gracious."

"You were wonderful. Hell, you even let me steer the plane for a while."

He puts his hand on my shoulder and offers a warm smile. "There's nothing like flying."

When I return I notice the Miracle has separated from the festivities and is staring out a window into the darkness with a drink in her hand. I wander over and attempt to give her a hug but she brushes me off. Is she in a funk? When I ask her what's the matter, she is at a loss to explain and pushes me away.

A little alarmed I begin to discreetly observe her as she appears to be giving our host Jack Daniels a run for his money in the race to consume the most alcohol.

Uh-oh...

After more conversation around the table, Livingston turns to me. "JD tells me you went to Berklee College of Music."

"Yes, a long time ago."

He smiles. "Then let's go play a few tunes."

We take turns playing the piano and singing, doing a little harmony, and just plain having fun. Once in a while one of us will play the guitar while the other guy stays on the keys.

Around midnight, we decide to call it a night, slap a couple of high fives, and head for what's left of the blueberry pie.

The music has even inspired Jack Daniels to stay awake and remain relatively coherent. "Man, what a magical evening." Jack raises a glass. "In my next life I must learn to play an instrument. Thank you both. We're going to have a wonderful summer."

I slap JD a high five. "What a joyride. Hey Jack, have you seen the Miracle?"

He thinks for a few seconds. "I believe she's outside talking to that impressive-looking young sailor dude. Be careful, or she may ditch you for him, though I think your music makes you a keeper."

I wander out back to find my girl talking to the guy and suddenly get a sick feeling in my stomach, like the odd man out. She's completely hammered and slurs to me, "We're having a good talk. Will you please leave us?"

The guy is nice and says, "He can stay. We were just talking about the charm of the Vineyard."

After a few awkward moments, she wanders off in search of more booze and I take in the fabulous stars with the young man.

I look up. "What a night. The skies here are just so clear." I point to a thick cluster in the distant sky. "You can even see the Milky Way."

He looks across the endless sky. "It's mind blowing... 'Silently, one by one, in the infinite meadows of heaven, blossomed the lovely stars, the forget-me-nots of the angels.' Amen."

"Beautiful. Did you just come up with that?"

He smiles. "No, that's Longfellow. Every once in a while that English degree comes in handy. The sky is luminous."

"To think people used to travel the seas navigating with these celestial bodies as their guides is crazy."

"They were either courageous or foolish." He laughs.

"Perhaps both..."

"Hey man, the music tonight with Livingston was awesome. Thank you."

I pat his shoulder. "Thank you."

"The Vineyard is definitely special."

I turn toward him. "Do you live here?"

He shakes his head. "No, just passing through for the weekend. How about you?"

"She and I are here for the season. We watch this house during the week while the owners are down in New York."

He appears momentarily stunned. "Oh, so you two came up here together? I had no idea."

"Yes, we drove up from Nashville. We just arrived last week, and I hope the two of us can stay intact until the end of August. OK, maybe the end of July... hell the end of the week. What were you saying about being foolish and courageous?"

The two of us wander back inside. There is no sign of her. I take a look out front and find she has cornered poor Livingston by his car.

Oh Lord...

It's late and I'm tired, so I hug the rest of what's left of the party goodnight and head off to bed. At some point in the middle of the night, she climbs in next to me.

Chapter 16

"The angry words spoken in haste
Such a waste of two lives
It's my belief pride is the chief cause, in the decline
Of the number of husbands and wives"
Roger Miller

The next morning I share an early espresso with Jack Daniels on one of his decks overlooking the Elizabeth Islands. The breeze carries the fragrance of the sea up to our lofty perch. An osprey hovers over a large pond looking for some breakfast.

JD sighs. "God, what a view! Now if we could just figure out a way to get rid of the Evil Queen, we would be home free."

I smile and raise my coffee mug. "What if you sent her abroad?"

He shakes his head. "She would never go for it. Her greatest joy in life is making me miserable."

"I guess everyone has their calling." I look out over our exquisite paradise. "I'm not sure I've said it enough, but thanks for having us."

"You're most welcome." He toasts my mug with his. "This place is something else, and for me personally, I love sharing it. But our three kids never come visit, so it's mostly just us, and you see how well that works."

He makes me laugh. "You're funny. Ever consider comedy?"

Jack D shakes his head. "I wish. No, I did what my old man wanted me to do, which was finance. It was all

about making the dinero. Always was, always will be...
Hey, somebody has to pay for all of this." He points
across his property and then down toward his wife in
the garden. "And cover the bills for that piece of shit
down there watering the weeds. No, I sold my soul to
Wall Street a long time ago and there's no buying it
back."

"Well, if your hedge fund ever tanks, I still think
you could thrive on the comedy circuit."

"You think? Hey, incredible music last night."

"Livingston is a gifted talent."

"You held your own, too. I like the way you guys
sounded together. The house comes alive with
music." A rich sea breeze passes over us. He takes a
deep breath and exhales slowly. "So, did you actually
write a book?"

"Yes. I think I got a couple of the test pressings
back today. My dad called last night to say a package
showed up at the cabin for me."

"You better make sure I get a copy. How is your
old man?"

"He's doing well for a poor kid from Brooklyn. I
love him; he's been good to me."

"You're a lucky bastard to have him around. Mine
died a long time ago. He was a Brooklyn boy too;
worked his ass off and died way too young. He was one
tough bastard and didn't have a lot of nice things to say,
but I wish he could have seen all this." He sweeps his
hand across the horizon.

"What a shame. Did he get to appreciate any of
your success?"

JD shakes his head. "Not really. Most of this came
after he passed. He never saw my kids grow up
either. We did have a couple of nice moments right

102

before he died. In his way, I knew he loved me, but God forbid he could have ever said it."

I'm shocked to see Jack Daniels's eyes filled with tears. I put my hand on his shoulder. "He would have been proud of you."

"We'll never know... Hey, what did you put in this coffee, truth serum? I never share this kind of stuff. Whatever you do, don't tell her." He casts a leery eye down at the Evil Queen. "If she senses any weakness, she'll gut me."

"Your secrets are safe with me, cowboy."

He reaches out to shake my hand. "Thank you, sir. We men need to stick together."

Two hours later, the Miracle and I are cruising back to Edgartown in a very quiet car.

I break the ice.

"So, my dear, any thoughts about last night?"

"The music was fabulous."

"I'm surprised you remember it. Anything else?"

Long silence. "I drank too much... again."

More empty space.

"You got anything else?"

"I'm sorry..."

A long and awkward silence lingers over the remainder of the ride, leaving plenty of space for my thoughts to take wing.

As much as I love the woman next to me, I can't live like this; it is too taxing and circular. I don't want to give up and quit on us, but what are my options, my choices? Apologies are essential, yet if the behaviors don't change, what's the use? Where is the personal responsibility? How do you help someone who doesn't think she needs assistance?

It's fabulous being back on the Vineyard. Why can't she just relax, have fun, and enjoy our blessings? This time should be a celebration and not feel like a wake.

She interrupts my mind stream. "I think I'm picking up the hostile vibrations from the house, and it's affecting my choices. Remember how sensitive I am."

"You're intuitive, but—"

"Last night I started feeling all this random anger and frustration, and then began drinking whiskey. I never drink hard liquor; it makes me mean and I hate it." I glance over and see she's staring out her window at the passing fields. "I don't know if I can stay there. Maybe we can rent something just for us."

"You make the place sound like something out of an Edgar Allan Poe poem."

"Those two despise each other, and trust me on this: the hostile energy permeates and affects us."

I can't help but notice that at first the mall was to blame, then the job and now it's the mansion. I'm sure it will be me next, or anything or anyone except the person in the mirror.

However, she does have a point about the energy between them being tough. They are toxic, but they will be gone 95% of the time.

What's really scary is if the Miracle is this sensitive, she and I may have to live in a Buddhist monastery to have any chance of making it. Which begs the question: will I have to eat brown rice for the rest of my life?

"Pauly, did you hear me?"

"Yes, love. I was just thinking about what you said. Luckily they're leaving this afternoon and we won't see them for three weeks, which buys us some time. You know, I actually had some nice moments with

Jack Daniels this morning and he's not that bad. So far they have been generous to open their home to us."

"But the energy of the place is so harsh."

We pass the airport and the part of me that loves to quit and run whispers in my ear, 'just pull right in there and drop her off. All of your troubles will be behind you and you can relax and enjoy the summer. For a moment this option is tempting. After all this is a deeply held reflex. Yes, I quit before, but not this time. I decide to hang tough and not flee emotionally.

"Pauly, did you hear what I said?"

I steal a sideways glance her way. "Yes, love. Their dynamic is tough, yes." I silently consider a few options. Should we give up and go home? But what about the book? I don't want to give up on her or my literary baby.

I glance toward her. "Let's not run the white flag up the pole just yet. I'll get a Vineyard Gazette and we can start looking for a spot in town. But be warned: it is July and finding something affordable is going to be tough. This is the peak season and it runs straight through the middle of August."

She leans over and kisses my cheek. "Thanks for hearing me. You will manifest something. You always do."

An hour later, we are in the Parental Asylum and I'm holding the very first copy of my memoir. It is a strange feeling, almost an out-of-body experience: my book...

Really? My book?

Yes, indeed. And to think it originated from my mysterious dream to become a third dimensional piece of soft cover stardust. Wild...

The Miracle is even happier than me. "You did it, Pauly! I am so proud of you. This is only the start. You watch..."

My mom is sitting at the kitchen table reading from another copy.

"In the summer of 1974, Steven Spielberg and I arrived in Martha's Vineyard. I came for a family vacation; he came to shoot the movie 'Jaws.' Which I assumed, given the title, was about my mother."

My Dad laughs out loud.

Mom gives us both a trenchant look. "Hey, that's not funny!"

Dad laughs again. "I'm sorry, but remember this is satire." He puts his palm next to his mouth and delivers a false whisper to Mom. "But call our lawyer and tell him to change the will."

I laugh. "Poetic justice." Max waddles in to see what the commotion is about and I give him a gentle pet.

"Don't hurt him," Mom says.

"I'll be careful."

The Miracle gives me a look like she's biting her tongue, trying not to laugh.

Mom continues reading.

"The Parental Asylum sits nestled at the dead end of a dirt road, so there's never much traffic. With its cedar walls, the place is rustic and down home. Mom's choice of decorating motif: Early American Cluttered. The counters and walls are covered in a variety of garage sale nick-knacks (i.e., General Robert. E. Lee Memorial Tea Set, a tattered map of Armenia, a list of Reader's Digest Top-Ten Jigsaw Puzzles, old pictures of Clark Gable).

I point towards what looks like an old ice pick. "Hey Mom, what's this?"

"Oh be careful with that. I bought it a couple of years ago at the Bishop's garage sale. It's a Pope Pius XII pick ax."

I kiss my mom on the cheek and turn to my cohort. "Miracle, why don't we bring a couple of these down into town and see if we can use your good looks to help us get a few of them in the bookstore?

She smiles. "We can try. Let me get my purse."

With the Miracle by my side and the book in hand, I float down the streets of Edgartown like Gene Kelly in *Singing In The Rain.* Turning a corner, I run right into the celebrated author, David McCullough (*Truman, 1776, John Adams*). He happens to be accompanied by his lovely wife, Rosalee.

"Hey there, what do you say?" Mr. McCullough's deeply resonant voice is easily recognizable to anyone who has ever turned on PBS, or watched the fabulous Ken Burns series, *The Civil War.*

After introductions all around, King David asks, "Are you still playing the piano up there at the old hotel?" He points up North Water Street in the direction of the Harborview.

"Not anymore. I remember you coming up some nights and singing quite a few standards."

"I'm an abominable singer," the King says with candor.

Rosalee smiles. "But he loves to sing more than anything." I can sense in her an exceptional kindness, a calm knowing and peace.

"David, those evenings were so much fun. No, I haven't performed there in years."

"Well, what are you doing with yourself these days?"

Should I say anything about the object in my hand? What the hell...

"It's funny you ask." I feel a little sheepish, but the boulder's rolling down the hill. "I just got the proof back from my first book." I hold it up for the King's inspection.

"How terrific! Way to go! Hey Rosalee, look, his first book." He shakes my hand warmly. I hand the book to him and he looks it over. "*Hitchhiking With Larry David.* How fabulous! But I have one question: who the hell is Larry David?"

I laugh out loud and so does the Miracle. "He created the program *Seinfeld*, and also has a show on HBO called *Curb Your Enthusiasm.*"

"Well, I can't say I've seen those." (A fellow non-TV watcher?) "But may I read it?"

There's no way to tell the King 'no' so I try to gracefully backpedal out of what is surely a polite request from the two-time Pulitzer prize-winning literary giant. "How kind, but you don't have to..."

David insisting, "Nonsense, I would love to read it."

"Well... I..."

The King goes farther: "Why don't you come up to the house this weekend, and we will sit and catch up?"

(Is this happening?) "Ah, should I call first?"

"No, just come up. We'll be home. Right, honey?" He turns to his longtime soul mate.

"Absolutely," she says.

"I should call first."

Rosalee gently touches me on my hand. "Just come up."

While I am still considering all this, the King just decides. "It's done then. See you on Saturday."

Wait, you have my book! I think. Ah, maybe we...

Chapter 17

"How wonderful it is
That nobody need wait a single moment
Before starting to improve the world."
Anne Frank

A few days later, I am moving eight hundred of my books into a small storage facility near the airport. "You know, sweet pea, if we are lucky enough to sell any of these, we can use the money for rent and fancy dinners."

The Miracle looks up. "I could use a nice hat to block the sun."

"As long as you get it at the thrift store."

"Don't even joke..."

"I wasn't..."

We throw a few boxes into the back of our Prius and activate our elaborate distribution plan, which in layman's terms means: anyone who says yes.

First stop: the Edgartown Bookstore, where we encounter a skeptical owner. "You wrote this and published it? We don't ever take these kind of things." He looks it over. "Is this a true story?"

"Every word of it."

"I see Larry endorsed it. I don't know..."

Time to throw the old Hail Mary. "Here, just take five of them, don't give me a dime, and if they don't sell in a week or two, I'll come back and get them. Hell, I'll even buy something from you. So there is no risk involved..."

He ponders. "OK, what the hell. Just give me five of them, and leave your number to come get them if they tank. There's no reason to go through a lot of rigmarole."

We shake hands and depart.

The Miracle states the obvious. "Boy, talk about tough."

"I hope the hat you want costs about a dollar."

She laughs. "One book at a time, Pauly, one at a time."

"At least we discovered the secret formula: zero down and no payments for ninety years."

"Oh Pauly..."

The two of us then canvas the island and end up with about six locations. With the sales staff feeling fried, we head over to Lucy Vincent Beach for a long swim.

The young gatekeeper recognizes me as I hand him my papers. He emanates suspicion. "So you have a pass this year? How did you score that? Do I need to check and see if this is stolen? So no more sneaking on..."

"My papers are in order, along with sincere promises of no more beach skullduggery. Like I told you last summer, Fredo, in five years the Corleone Family will be completely legit."

He smiles and does not miss a beat. "It is just business, Sonny, don't take it personally."

I'm grinning as well. "So you love *The Godfather* films too?"

"Nothing beats *Parts One* and *Two*. It's good to see you again."

"Hey, here's a gift for you for being so cool last year." I hand him a copy of *HHLD*.

He checks it out. "I love Larry David. I heard he is lurking about, though I've been coming here for years and have yet to see him.

The Miracle says, "Well just hang around this character and he's bound to turn up. In fact he's probably in the car behind us."

The guard smiles. "So did you write this?"

"I did. So don't throw it in the trash bin until our car is safely out of sight."

"No dude, I'll check it out. Thank you."

We park the car, take a long walk down the shore to the 'clothing optional' section, and set up camp. A moment later I am stripped bare and sprinting into the water. "It's freezing! Oh my God! Now I'll never have children."

"Pauly, you're naked!"

"I am? I had no idea. Quick, bring me my clothes."

After a moment's hesitation, the Miracle wanders in topless and, despite the chill, we enjoy the water. I point toward the dunes.

"Last summer I used to sit right there and miss you terribly. Thank God we ended up back together."

"Yes, let's never be apart again."

"Deal."

We hug on it.

A few sun-kissed hours at Lucy Vincent does the trick. "I feel so much better here," the Miracle says. "This is such a glorious stretch of beauty."

"Amen, my love."

With the daylight beginning to fade, we drive out and come upon the same guard reading my gift.

He holds up the book. "Man, this is terrific. Thank you. Can I buy one for my girlfriend's father? He would love this."

I'm kind of shocked. "Sure! They're twenty dollars."

"Will you sign it?" He hands me the twenty. "And sign mine also. Super funny, dude, and this shit is deep. You're making me think. Thank you."

I get the names straight and start signing. "Are you kidding? Thank you for making my day." I hold up the cash. "And now we have pizza money."

I turn to the Miracle. "The hat can wait, right?"

She shakes her head. "Oh stop it..."

We grab a couple of slices on the old wooden porch at the Chilmark Store and watch the sunburned patrons come and go. After a couple of cold peach slushies, I turn to her and say, "If we leave now we might catch the last of the pink afterglow from one of our balconies."

As we pull into the driveway, my cellphone rings. It's the Edgartown Bookstore. I look at the Miracle. "Shit. I bet he changed his mind."

"You have to answer it."

I reluctantly do so. "Hello?"

"Paul, this is the bookstore. We sold all five of your books in a couple of hours. I put them out on the front wall and they flew off the shelf."

I get goose bumps and put my hand over the phone. "They sold all the books!"

"Pauly... how incredible!"

I take my hand off the phone and ask, "Do you want some more?"

"Of course. Why don't you bring me a box, and this time sign them. Oh, and I have a check for you. By the way, you totally nailed the 'I'm Robin Cook' chapter. When you come down here, I'll share a few of my own Cook stories... if you promise not to print them."

"I promise!"

After I hang up, the Miracle and I do a dance around the pool and then unwind in the hot tub while watching the stars show up in the clear night sky.

The next evening we are walking through Edgartown eating ice cream cones when an elegant woman with a lovely young girl says, "I hate to intrude, but did you write that wonderful book with the thumb on the cover?"

"I did. When did you buy one of the very first copies?"

"Yesterday. It moved me and I couldn't put it down. My husband is back at the hotel reading it now. Oh my God, is this the Miracle?"

"In all her glory."

She shakes her hand. "I am so happy you guys are still together. By the end of the book, I was so rooting for you. Oh, I'm sorry—my name is Lynn, and this is my daughter."

"Hello. You two angels made our night."

"No, you made ours. I usually would never bother anyone, but when I thought it was you, well, I had to say something. We come here every year from Newtown, Connecticut.

The Miracle bends down and asks the little girl, "What's your name?

The girl looks down, then up. "Grace." Then she shares, "I want to live here someday."

"You do?" The Miracle says, "That sounds wonderful. We want to live here too."

The girl is shy at first, but slowly opens up. With her blond hair, blue eyes, and tanned skin, she's adorable. "I also want to write a book one day. And have my pictures in it."

I look at the little angel. "Hey, if I can do it, anyone can."

Lynn looks up at me. "The part about you almost drowning was deeply moving."

Grace says, "Mom read to me the part about the magic girl and the big horse. That was my favorite."

"How old are you, sweet child?"

Grace crunches up her forehead. "I'm six and next year I will be in the first grade."

"Well, I'm so overwhelmed. I may need to get a second ice cream cone to celebrate."

They laugh, and the Miracle gives me a playful nudge. "No you don't; I think you are fat enough."

"She's right. All we do is eat."

The Miracle adds, "But in reality, I'm the only one who gains any weight. It's not fair. He never gains a pound."

I look stricken. "Because I'm riddled with parasites."

Grace's eyes go wide. "Really?"

Lynn grins. "No, honey, he's kidding." She says to the Miracle. "I can't believe how gorgeous you are."

She blushes. "You're kind."

I put my hand on the Miracle's shoulder. "I tell her every day, but she won't believe me."

We all hug it out and go our separate ways. As we walk up the street towards the car, the Miracle turns to me and says, "This is fun!"

"It is, and we were even touched by Grace."

Chapter 18

"What does a man need? Really need?
A few pounds of food each day, heat and shelter
Six feet to lie down in and some form of working activity
That will yield a sense of accomplishment
That's all – in the material sense, and we know it
But we are brainwashed by our economic system
Until we end up in a tomb"
Sterling Hayden

When Saturday rolls around the Miracle and I head down the road to share some time with the McCullough Clan. Their West Tisbury house is a modest, classic white colonial from the past century sitting right off the main street. The front door is open so I tap gingerly on the light screen frame.

A sonorous voice shouts, "Come in."

Did he say come in? Or... Can I just arrive unannounced and waltz into David McCullough's house?

You can't do that.

"David..?"

"Yes, come in."

OK then, here we go. I feel a bit nervous at first but the Good Queen Rosalee puts us both quickly at ease.

After some small talk, I take advantage of these privileged circumstances and ask, "David, did you always want to be a writer?"

"No, but once I got the bug I had to do it. I didn't want to be one of those old guys standing around the water cooler talking about something I was going to write one of these days."

Rosalee interjects. "I remember he came home and said 'I have to quit my job and pursue the writing or I'll never know if I am any good.' So I said of course."

He points at her. "She backed me unconditionally, and keep in mind: we had five children to feed."

The Miracle asks her. "Were you concerned?"

She shakes her head slightly. "I didn't think too much about it, because I totally believed in him. I felt no matter what he decided to do, he would be successful."

The Miracle and I look at each other and shake our heads. I ask him, "David, were you afraid?"

He doesn't miss a beat. "Heavens, I was terrified. But I wasn't going to let that stop me."

"Were you ever worried?"

"Only every single day."

I laugh out loud. "How honest."

"Well, I was. But you can't let fear and worry stand in the way of doing what you want to do. You have to live your dream. You cannot cower in the shadows. You have to give it all you have, and never give up. Remember, I only *made it* a few years ago when a couple of my pieces were turned into television programs. My financial success is only a recent phenomenon. Of course, it helps to have someone like her supporting you."

Rosalee beams. "Isn't he wonderful."

He is. I say, "You two have something transcendent of what most people would call success. You have true love."

"You are very kind," she says humbly.

The Miracle puts her hand in mine. "Actually, it is inspiring. When did you two know you wanted to get married? Was it love at first sight?"

"I knew right away," Rosalee says. "We got fixed up on a date, and then he came up here to the island to see me. My family, the Barnes clan, has been coming here for ages. I remember when we used to ride horses down Barnes Road into Oak Bluffs."

David jumps in. "I came up to the Vineyard to see her that summer and I knew I wanted to marry her. But I wasn't sure she wanted to have me."

She smiles. "Oh, he knew. It's been a wonderful adventure together."

Then David says, almost to himself. "It certainly has passed rather quickly."

There is a serene moment of divine stillness as the four of us ponder this. The scent of freshly cut grass drifts through the open windows and dances amongst us. I look up on the wall at a series of photographs capturing so many of their life moments.

Finally, David reaches down and holds up HHLD. "I loved this. I read it all in one sitting; it was fabulous. You have a gift."

Rosalee says, "Actually, I read it first, over two days, and it was hard to put down. I said to him, 'David, you need to read this, it is enchanting and inspiring."

David smiles and gets a twinkle in his eye. "And believe me, I listen to her when she says something like that. I hope this is the first of many works."

This exchange has done the impossible: render me speechless.

The Miracle laughs. "He is stunned into silence."

"What can I say, other than thank you both so much? You just made my summer, and maybe even my fall, winter, next spring..."

He chuckles. "You're clever and you have a flair for humor. Writing funny is not easy. I could never write humorously, but you had me laughing out loud in several sections."

Rosalee leans forward in her chair. "I've been afraid to ask, but I have to know." She turns toward the Miracle. "Are you the girl he writes about so eloquently?"

"Yes I am."

There is a sense of relief and laughter all around.

"We wondered... and how gratifying to know there was a happy ending. I hope you two will stay together."

"This is our goal," the Miracle laughs. "But I don't know with this one."

I hold my hands up. "I am a changed man. I have renounced my wicked ways and I'm on record as reformed, right there in those pages."

As we bask in the glow of their loving sanctuary I feel as though the room is filled with joy and light.

David jumps up. "Hey, Piano Man, how about playing a couple of songs for old time's sake?"

Rosalee says to the Miracle. "The man loves to sing."

I've learned you don't say 'no' to King David, so I sit at the piano and take us up and down Broadway. David sings his heart out...

You must remember this
A kiss is still a kiss
A sigh is just a sigh
The fundamental things apply
As time goes by...

I have not run into many folks who love to croon as much Mr. Two Pulitzer Prizes. You can't help but get caught up in his enthusiasm.

Finally, it is time for us to depart. Lots of hugs are exchanged.

"Promise us you will come again and come often," Rosalee insists.

The Miracle says, "We will," and I confirm.

As we pull away from their home they wave to us from the front door. The Miracle turns to me and says, "I have never been in a home filled with more love. They are impressive. We are so lucky to have spent time with them. What a love story. Pauly, can we create one as enthralling as theirs?"

I smile and give her a kiss on the cheek. "We already have."

Chapter 19

"You will find
That many of the truths we cling to
Depend greatly on our own point of view."
Obi-Wan Kenobi

The Oak Bluffs Paper Store sits at the heart of the town's constant hustle and bustle. The joint is a small place packed to the gills with all the summer essentials: sunscreen, gum, water pistols, soda, newspapers, pain relievers... you name it, they have it.

One sunny day I wander in like Willy Loman and spy a guy about my age standing behind the counter. "May I speak to the person in charge?"

"You're looking at him. How can I help you?"

I hold up a copy of HHLD. "This is mine, and I was wondering if you would consider carrying a couple copies?"

He glances at me briefly and then the book. "Sure. I'd love to."

"Wow. If only everything in life was that easy."

"Amen, brother. Let me get an extra copy for myself. I could use a healthy distraction."

"Here, take one on me."

"No, I'm happy to pay you."

"Please. I insist."

"OK then, thank you." He sticks out his hand. "I'm Luke."

We shake hands. "So this is your store?"

"This place has been in my family for three generations. My grandfather started it, then my dad ran it for a number of years, before I took the reins."

I look around at the place. "What a legacy. In 1976 my brother and I bought some candy here as kids, and then walked down the street to the theater and watched a movie called *Star Wars*."

He smiles. "I might have been there that night. What an awesome film." He glances over my shoulder at the store. "There is a lot of history in this place for me and my family, and many others like yourself."

"Use the Force, Luke..." I say in my best Obi-Wan voice. "Luke Store Walker. Sorry, I couldn't resist."

"Yes, Master..."

There are times when you meet someone new and it's like picking up right where you once left off. There is an ease of connection, a flow, a familiarity, and fellowship that transcends the linear circumstances.

"Here are the books, and my card if lightning strikes and a few of them sell. If not, we will have some good kindling come fall."

He chuckles, and I exit back into the Oak Bluffs throng.

A couple days later, I get a call from Luke Store Walker.

"Well, I don't know about lightning, but all of them sold in two days."

"I'm shocked. How many books did you buy?"

"Actually two, and it's a fabulous read. So please bring me another box. In fact, make it two. I'm going to keep it up on the counter."

"The HHLD Delivery Department prides itself on excellent service. So I will be right over."

Thirty minutes later, I am on my way there along my favorite Vineyard sojourn. As the light softly dances between the clouds, I slowly wind the Prius out of Edgartown and up the beach road. With the Nantucket Sound on my right and Sengekontacket Pond on the left, I'm surrounded by water.

I pop in and catch Luke unpacking some boxes and putting a variety of merchandise on the shelves. He greets me warmly with a handshake and a big smile. "I love your writing."

"I never get tired of hearing kind words."

He smiles. "Thanks for bringing me some more stock. The first batch sold to all kinds of people. Old, young, white, black, tourist, resident; it was a broad demographic."

I try to process this, but can only shake my head. "What inspires me are these wonderful notes I have been receiving."

"Well, in a way, your perspective gives people permission, since you were so open in the book."

"What an interesting take."

He glances up at me. "So, I have to ask." Luke leans forward a little. "Are you with the Miracle?"

"The question many ask..."

He puts his right hand on his heart. "Well, after reading your words, you sort of fall in love with the two of you."

I feel my own heart tug. "What a kind thing to say. Thank you."

"I mean it. It is apparent you love her."

"I do, deeply. Yet I often find myself wondering why it can't be as simple as two people who love each other living happily ever after?"

"Well I've been married for over ten years, my friend, and relationships are complex creatures."

"There are days when I feel completely lost in terms of how to cope with certain things." I ponder whether to share about her drinking, but it feels like I would be betraying her privacy, so I abstain. "Hopefully it's just a stage we're moving through."

He looks me in the eye. "You can always find me here if you need a shoulder."

"Thanks, brother." I make an effort to shake off my funk and shift the subject. "Have you always worked in the store?"

"Yes. First, as a kid growing up and then, off and on through college. I took a break when I began practicing law in the big city."

"An attorney?"

He laughs. "I hated it. So after killing myself for a few years trying to make partner, I walked away and came back here to a simpler life. The store has its moments, but for the most part I love it. I live about a mile away, so I can go home and have lunch with my family. Quality of life, brother; it's all that matters."

"You're preaching to the choir." I point at a picture on the wall. "You as a boy?"

Luke saddens. "With my dad. " He looks away and then down. "I miss him. He was a good man who died much too young."

"I'm sorry."

He pauses for a moment. "I found him... you know? He didn't come in one morning, which was a first, so I went over to the house to check, and he was lying on the front porch as cold as a stone. I'll never get over that moment."

He takes a few deep breaths and I let him just be with it.

After a moment or two, he returns to fussing with the new stock. "How about you? Is your Dad still with us?"

"Yes, he is and I am going straight from here to give him a long hug... and maybe a couple of donuts."

"You are very lucky. I remember reading where you two were having trouble connecting. I hope things have improved."

"They have, radically. I will tell you: it's been tough to watch him age. And my Mom, too... They were once like gods, but now I see them as mere mortals like myself."

"Go home and hug him. Then tell him how much you love him, because one day you'll no longer be able to. I've learned to never leave love unspoken. Life is too short and much too fragile."

Chapter 20

"Sometimes the questions are complicated
And the answers are simple."
Dr. Seuss

I walk in and find my parents at the kitchen table poring over a partially completed jigsaw puzzle.

"Hey guys, is that George Washington?"

My Mom looks up. "No, Betty White. We got this for a nickel at a garage sale."

"Can I give you both a big hug?"

Mom says, "Of course you can."

Dad smiles, gets up slowly. "If you insist." As I hug my dad, Luke's words ring through my ears.

Dad gives me a squeeze. "It's good having you here."

"I love you, Dad."

"I love you too, son."

Mom feigns offense. "What about me?"

I give her another hug. "We love you too."

I reach down and pet Max. "Good boy."

"Don't hurt him," my mother recites.

What could I possibly say at this point?

My mom looks up at me. "Your brother just called. He and his wife are coming up this weekend." She finds a piece of Betty White's forehead and taps it into place. "I hate to say it, but it's a shame he's bringing her. You know, in all these years she has never called me once. I have left messages, sent cards, even gifts, but nothing comes back in return." Her face brightened. "Oh, here's the piece I was looking for."

Dad says, "It just feels more relaxed when she doesn't come. She just sits in the room most of time, and she never smiles."

"Well, with the two of them here, the Miracle and I will have to get a room in town for the weekend. I think it will be too crowded around the cabin."

Dad looks at me suspiciously. "You're trying to avoid her, aren't you?"

"It's just easier and less awkward. Her energy is tough for me." I get a glass and fill it with water. "If it makes you feel any better, she treats me the same way. Chris says it's not personal."

Mom looks up from the partial gaze of Betty White. "Do you believe Chris?"

"I actually do; he has never been a liar. Hey, he loves her and it works for them, so what else matters? For me personally, it's a shame, but it is what it is."

Dad gives me another hug. "Where are you going with the snorkel bag?"

"Over to the beach for my daily swim."

He looks alarmed. "Didn't you read that there are a whole bunch of great white sharks across Nantucket Sound roaming the cape looking for seals? Are you sure you want to go in the water?"

"They're looking for seals, not bald guys. Besides, I have to go. I can't let the fear keep me out of the ocean. But thanks to your warning, I'll now take my entire swim in about 18 inches of water."

"Are there any man-o-wars?"

"Stop it..!"

I flee the house.

~~~

A couple days later, I am strolling through Edgartown holding hands with the Miracle on the most perfect summer evening. "Sweet pea, should we get some ice cream?"

"Pauly, I have to stop eating so much."

My phone vibrates.

"Hello?"

"This is the Edgartown bookstore. Sorry to bother you this late, but we need a couple more boxes pronto."

"Oh? I already dropped two off earlier in the week."

"We sold those! Please bring some more. *Hitchhiking With Larry David* is our top-selling title this week, just barely ahead of *The Girl With The Dragon Tattoo*."

"That's insane!" I turn to the Miracle, give her the news and then go back to my call. "Okay, I have a few boxes in my car. Give me a couple minutes and I'll drop them off."

The Miracle gives me a warm, slow kiss on my cheek. "Way to go, Pauly. Hey, I'm going to look for that beach hat you promised me. Text me when you're done."

We hug and separate. After dropping off the boxes, I walk out on to Main Street and straight into a short bald man in his early sixties with a pair of thick glasses that make him look like the official spokesman for the National Nerd Society.

He lights up when he sees me. "Well, hello my friend. How is your summer going?"

We hug. "Billionaire Bob! I've been wondering where you were."

He shakes his head and looks a bit grim. "I had to have an operation on my heart. It put the fear of God into me but, knock on wood, everything is now one hundred percent."

"So you're okay?"

"Much better than I was before. How about you? My spies tell me you have a book out that is very popular. Though I heard there are some people down at the Yacht Club who are none too pleased." He points at the bookstore. "Do they have a copy of your book?"

"They do."

"Wait here. I'll get a few of them, and you can sign them for me. Good for you."

The quaint lamps illuminate the red brick sidewalks as I sit on a bench and watch an endless parade of summer people pass by. It looks like everyone is sunburned and licking an ice cream cone while looking into the windows of the tiny shops along Main Street.

There are lots of smiles and you can hear laughter in the air. I see fathers with little girls on their shoulders and grandparents holding hands. Some have come to this haven for generations to bond and reconnect during the season of leisure.

In a few minutes Billionaire Bob returns with ten of the just-delivered copies and has me sign them to various folks. He opens one up. "Am I in here?"

"You are, sir."

"Uh-oh..."

"No, I think you will be pleased."

"By the way, did I see you yesterday walking in town with a very striking woman? Is this by chance the same girl you were so desperately missing last summer?"

"You remembered our talks. I'm touched."

"Of course I did. So?"

"It is her, and we are back together."

"Congratulations on the girl and this." He takes a moment, turning the pages. "This is terrific news."

I feel a tug on my arm and turn to see a man with a familiar and friendly face. "When did you get here?"

He smiles and gives me a hug. "We arrived late this afternoon and came into town after dinner to look around. Man, the streets are packed."

"The August crowds have arrived and it's only late July." Introductions are made and I ask his partner, "How are you doing?"

"Fine" is the flat one word response.

He chats with us for a couple minutes then says, "Let's catch up soon. I think we're going to walk down and get some ice cream. I love you."

I hug him one more time. "I love you too. I'm glad you're here; it's been a while."

The two of them wander off down Main Street towards the water. After a few moments, Billionaire Bob breaks the silence. "So is that your brother?"

"It is."

"Sweet guy, but what's with his wife. Do you two not like each other?"

My head jerks a little as if slightly jolted. "What makes you say that after such a brief meeting on the street?"

He measures his words. "Remember, I read people every day for a living. It's the only way to make anything happen in my crazy world. First thing was, her body language. And then, she never said a single word to either of us, there was no eye contact, and she kept tugging on his arm like a nervous dog pulling on a leash. Obviously, she couldn't walk away fast enough."

I think my mouth is hanging open before I say, "Keep going; I'm impressed."

"Her energy was absent, and there was a complete lack of engagement. And though it was subtle, he started to rush his words... as if he was beginning to feel

131

a bit awkward... and then he semi-abruptly ended his story and the encounter."

"Wow Bob, I'm speechless."

"When did you last see him?"

I think for a second. "Well over a year ago."

"If I was seeing my brother for the first time after a year, I would have been much more warm and embracing. Definitely not so measured and reserved, and I certainly would not walk away after just a couple of minutes. He also didn't invite us, or you, to join them for ice cream. What happened?"

I take and release a deep breath. "Nothing ever happened. That's the odd thing. There was no blow up or fight with her. She's just been like this towards me, and everyone in the family, since day one. Yet he doesn't see it."

"He loves her, and probably just doesn't want to deal with it. Remember he sees you once a year, but lives with her every day. It's a shame, but don't take it personally. Heck, don't take anything personally."

"The zen of Billionaire Bob. Your wise words will be heeded. Thank you, Master."

He turns to leave, then suddenly looks back. "Hey, are we going to have coffee one morning this week before I head back to Ireland?"

I grin. "Only if you let me buy."

"Don't be silly! You're only a poor writer. Speaking of which," he holds up the book, "I have some homework to do before we meet. And remember, until then don't tell any of my secrets."

I cross my heart. "Never!"

My phone rings. It's the Miracle. "Did you forget me?"

"How could I ever, even for an instant..."

"Pauly, please come down to The Great Put On at the end of Main and give me your opinion on a couple of items as soon as you can. And no stopping to pet any dogs or talk to your fans or well-wishers. You need me there to herd you. I miss you."

"Yes Master, and I miss you too."

A moment later, I am looking at her in a super sexy top, a tight white sheer number that fits her curves perfectly.

"Pauly, do you like it?"

"Are you kidding? I love it. How about the hat you were looking for?"

She puts on one that is both chic and stunning. To her credit, she has superb taste, and of course, everything appears to be made for her. "Can I get both, please?"

"Absolutely."

She then wanders over to a rack and picks up a winsome piece of black lingerie. "Should we get this too?"

"Is that a rhetorical question?"

We walk to the front of the store and put her choices on the counter. "Oh, I ran into my brother Chris. He looked quite fit."

She smiles. "I can't wait to see him. Was he alone?"

"No, she was with him."

"Any warmth?"

"All the charm of an iceberg."

"Well, take me back to the hotel and I will melt some ice and more. You have been a very good boy, and I want you to know what positive reinforcement feels like."

Chapter 21

"Let us be like
Two falling stars in the day sky.
Let no one know of our sublime beauty
As we hold hands with God
And burn
Into a sacred existence that defies -
That surpasses
Every description of ecstasy
And love."
Hafiz

The next day we lay motionless on a deserted strip of beach under a cloudless sky. We have both been in the water several times, and the sun's radiance feels like heaven on my skin.

She leans over and kisses my ear. "Did you have fun last night?"

I turn my head and kiss her. "You charge me in ways I have never experienced. Ours is the perfect combination of love and lust. You've spoiled me."

"You do it for me too. You're hot."

I gently kiss her cheek. "The chemistry has always been there, from the first moment."

She sighs. "But you didn't touch me for weeks when we met. I was convinced you were not romantically into me, which made me only want you more. We fit together, Pauly; it's not perfect, but nothing is. We have a celestial magic that is rare to find. Do you know how many men I have met?"

"I can't imagine."

She sits up a bit. "Too many to count, but no one has touched my soul like you have. You just get me, and I see you. It's rare, and I never thought I would find you, but thank God I did."

I touch her. "I'm in." A summer breeze passes over us. We are in the midst of a period of harmony and flow. Not perfect, but it's working. I am feeling a lot of love for the woman lying next to me.

I put my hand on her warm back. "You are always so magnificent to me, even on your worst days. I see your inner light and it is glorious."

"We chose each other. Our souls did." She smiles. "Pauly, let's go back and take a hot shower together. I want to look sexy for you and wear my new outfit to dinner tonight."

After another in an endless series of erotic summer showers, we walk hand in hand down to the Atlantic Restaurant and are greeted warmly at the door by my dear friend Jaime, the handsome, suave owner who runs the show with grace.

"You two are back! Oh my lord, how stunning is this ? Look at that tan, and those green eyes..." He comes out from behind the podium and kisses her hand, then hugs me.

"What, no kiss for me?" I joke.

"You play your cards right, mister, and you might just get a kiss, too."

"I know we waltzed in here last second on a busy Saturday night, so how long is the wait?"

"For you, there is never a wait." He points across the room to his assistant. "Take them to my favorite table by the water."

"Thank you," I say.

"Come on, my brother; you are family."

136

We are only at the table for a moment before a waiter arrives with a very expensive bottle of champagne. "This one is on Jaime. He says he loves you guys."

The Miracle smiles. "Please tell him we love him back."

The waiter pours and I toast. "To the love of my life."

"Ah, Pauly, you are my soul mate."

We take a sip and look out across the Edgartown Harbor. The light show is spectacular, and there are boats packed tightly on every mooring. A large sailboat silently passes with its sail in full bloom.

"My Miracle, how perfect is this vista?"

She looks like she might tear up. "I'm speechless. I can't wait until we have our own home here and children. Our life is going to be outstanding."

"It already is. I'm starving. How about you?"

She winces. "I'm going to nibble. I'm still feeling fat. I felt so self-conscious in my bikini today; thankfully, no one was around."

"Are you serious? In that provocative little black suit? I couldn't keep my hands off you."

The Miracle has always felt funny about her size. She is voluptuous and curvy, which works well for me since I've never found the emaciated skeleton look you see in all the fashion magazines to my liking. But no matter how many times I tell her how captivating she looks, it does not seem to penetrate her deep-seated doubt. I find it ironic, since she gets an insane amount of visual attention, almost to the point of annoyance.

"Pauly, you order and I'll figure something out."

As the sun slowly sets across the harbor, another sleek sailboat silently passes in the distance. My Ahi tuna arrives, but I'm feeling concerned, since the

Miracle is not eating, only pouring. "Remember, I only had a sip, so be careful or you will end up drinking the whole bottle yourself."

"We can't let Jaime's gift go to waste. Don't worry; I'll be fine." She pours what appears to be the last of it. "All done."

I take a bite and let the flavor seep into my being. "Are you sure you don't want any of this? It's fabulous."

She is looking down. Nothing... Did she hear me? Her answer, when it comes, is quite serious. "Can I be completely honest?"

I put down my fork. "Sure, what is it?"

"Well..." She takes a long sip and finishes her glass.

"Love, are you alright?"

She suddenly looks angry. "What do you mean? I'm fine. What was I saying?"

I think for just a few seconds. "You were going to be completely honest."

"Oh, right. Well, I feel like you never should have taken me out of San Diego to Nashville. I was too young, and you took advantage of me. It was wrong."

Her words cause me to fall into a deep farrago of feelings. With my mouth wide open, I try to process what I have just heard. Finally I say, "I'm stunned you feel this way." She says nothing, so I go on. "Do you remember my saying at the time that you should stay? But you literally begged me, for two months, to bring you back."

She holds up her empty glass and flags the waiter. "Say, can you bring me another glass of champagne?"

He acknowledges her request and scurries off.

138

"Hey, you've already had a bottle, and haven't eaten anything. Do you really think you need another glass?" My mood is plunging and taking my appetite along for the ride. You don't have to be clairvoyant to see where the night is headed.

My life suddenly feels like a bad television show and this is the evil twin episode. At some point the 'sweet' Miracle traded place with her evil twin before dinner and now I'm at the mercy of this monster.

"Don't tell me what to do. You can't control me. You are just like my father that way, so high and mighty. I know what you're trying to do here. And yes, I did ask or beg, maybe a lot, but you were older and wiser, Pauly, you should have said no. You knew better. I left everything for you. It was wrong."

I'm trying to remember if I have ever seen a human being make such a dramatic shift besides Linda Blair in *The Exorcist*. I feel an intense pain rising throughout my body and a knot growing in my stomach. "I... I don't know what... I mean..." I take a sip of water. "Well, it's never too late to go back." The waiter brings her drink and I quickly hand him my card so he will bring the check.

She rambles a bit and is sadly sloppy drunk and slurring her words, eventually circling back to... "But you shouldn't have brought me back. Pauly, it was wrong. You took me away. Why?"

The waiter returns and I sign the bill. It is time for me to escape this house fire as quickly as possible. I lean in and whisper, "Look, I love you, but I can't talk to you when you've been drinking. Especially in public at my friend's restaurant. Let's go back to the room or for a walk."

She raises her glass. "But I want to stay and have fun."

"You can, but I'm leaving." I stand up to leave. She starts to get up and spills some champagne on her new top.

"Shit, my blouse... hey, wait for me," she hisses.

I slowly walk her back to the room, but I realize there's no point in being with someone who has completely checked out. "I'm going out for some air. I'll see you when I get back."

"Fuck you. I won't be here when you get back. I'll find someone who wants to be with me."

Having lost all patience, I strike back. "Just be honest this time and warn the next victim you have a multiple personality disorder, among other endearing qualities. And look for someone from San Diego. It'll save me a ticket."

"Fuck you!"

This is the last thing I hear before fleeing.

My Lord, what a vile paradox: the compelling day, all the goodwill, and then dinner tonight. This enchanted summer is all going up in flames.

And why does this futile, heartbreaking exchange feel so familiar?

Then it hits me. I see my Aunt Joan, a hopeless alcoholic, blind drunk, berating my uncle and railing against the evil of men. He is the lightning rod for all the unrealized rage smoldering within her, eating away at her soul. I remember his empty resignation at a life slowly destroyed by drinking and spousal hate.

This is the same thing. I've seen this nightmare as a witness many times, and now I am in it.

In that moment something dies within me.

Without thinking, I stop in my tracks and sit down on the steps of the old red brick bank.

I know I can never be with her, let alone get married. We are done. Now it is just a matter of time until we bury the body.

She is right: I should never have brought her back. I knew it was wrong and I did it anyway.

I believed in her desperate pleas and declarations of blind love. I felt sorry for her, flat broke, bouncing between men and without a place to live.

Now what?

I sit in front of the bank and try to come to a little clarity. Yes, it's over now, but how to unwind it, and how quickly can this olive-skinned cancer be eradicated?

Maybe I will get lucky, and she will be gone when I get back, the bloated burden of the next fool.

A warm and familiar voice inquires, "Are you casing the joint for a heist?"

"Is it that obvious? Boy, you are a sight for sore eyes." I give my brother a long hug. "To answer your question, I am not. But since my date is completely inebriated and probably wandering the streets of Edgartown, I decided to sit here and ruin my one and only pair of dress pants."

My brother looks deeply concerned. "Oh, I'm sorry. How are you doing?"

Chris has always been a kind soul with a soft heart, beloved by all in our group and beyond. I don't think he has ever had an enemy. He's just one of those fortunate people who everyone always liked.

When God granted me a brother, I hit the lottery. We were inseparable for the first thirty years of our lives. Two guys living and breathing together in unison. But at some point, it must have been too much for him. He needed to break away, to create his own song. He had been a sideman long enough. His choice of a challenging wife only accelerated our separation.

It occurs to me to ask him why he is solo. "Chris, why are you walking around alone?"

"The wife wasn't feeling too well and went to bed early." He looks up at the heavens and then up the street. "It was such a lovely Vineyard evening I had to come down and soak it in. Do you mind if I join you?"

"Are you kidding? I would love it. It's rare we ever get any one-on-one time these days."

"I know. It's difficult, living so far apart. Would you like to walk around a little?"

I get up gingerly, dust off my backside and we proceed to stroll.

We park it in front of Mad Martha's Ice Cream Shop and he puts his hand on the front door and tilts his head to the side. "Can I buy you one for old time's sake?"

I notice my attitude has improved and my appetite is back. "What the hell, I mean, it does seems fitting."

The two of us grab a couple of cones and continue our walk down memory lane. Chris points at the bike shop. "Didn't you work there one summer for about five minutes?"

"More like five weeks."

"What happened?"

"I talked my way in, but after about three days the owner figured out I didn't know a thing about bikes and couldn't fix anything, even a cocktail."

He laughs. "You were always much more of an 'idea man.' How funny."

"He didn't know what to do with me so he put me up front. I mainly handled the money and told jokes. When I ran out of fresh comedic material, he had to let me go."

142

He smiles. "Showbiz is tough."

"Brutal. By the way this cookies and cream sugar cone is heaven-sent. Thank you."

He takes a lick of his. "So is mine. Ice cream in the Vineyard is always a good idea."

I point at two mopeds parked by the curb. "Now there's a memory."

He laughs. "It's funny now, but certainly wasn't then. Whatever you do, don't put that in one of your books."

Years ago my brother and I, along with two of our cousins, Ricky and Owen, 'borrowed' four mopeds. We rode all over the entire island until one of us got caught careening wildly through a farmer's field.

"Chris, what were we thinking?"

"Well," he says, considering, "obviously we weren't. We got caught up in our adolescent testosterone and trying to impress each other. But if I recall, Pauly, you got us off the hook."

I finish my cone and throw the napkin in a small can. "My first official gig as an attorney, and yes, I did."

"They were going to charge us with stealing the bikes, but you took the position that since the scooters never left the island, technically they were borrowed."

I laugh. "Luckily the police chief found the whole thing amusing and let us off with a slap on the wrist. We had to pay restitution of course but the real suffering came later from the in-house tribunal of pain, otherwise known as all of our parents."

He shakes his head. "Each of them trying to prove they were the stricter parent."

"It was like an auction where they kept bidding up our punishments higher and higher. It's funny now. Chris, what were you, like, twelve years old?"

"I think I was eleven, maybe even ten."

I laugh. "Mom thought we were headed for a life of crime and would wind up doing hard time. Thank God she didn't overreact, right?"

Chris laughs too, and then sobers up. "Hey, do you need to go check on your girl?"

I realize this beautiful encounter with my brother has completely taken my mind off the disaster which had been our dinner. "She's either back in the room sleeping it off, or quite possibly somewhere else tying one on."

Considering it all, I grimace. "Man, I joke but honestly my heart is breaking. Part of me feels numb, yet everything hurts. I feel clueless with her in terms of all of this. Sometimes I just want to take a long walk out there on the beach at night, fall to my knees and weep. It's humbling."

He looks into my eyes with empathy. "I am so sorry..."

"Hey, do you remember when Aunt Joan would get soused and have a super crazy look in her eyes? Almost like her being went black?"

"Yeah. Kind of like a rabid animal. Man, she would rail against the evils of men, as her husband Bob and the rest of us just sat there in silence. It was depressing... and there was nothing anyone could do once the rage started."

"I have to say, there have been a couple of times when the Miracle reminds me of all that."

"It's that bad? Brother, she needs help. Have you two ever talked about her going into some kind of rehab?"

"Yes, in an indirect way. I guess that's a conversation I've been semi-avoiding while hoping this whole thing magically works itself out. You're right though. It's something that needs to be addressed. I

144

mean, ultimately she needs my help, not my scorn. This is one of those 'for better or for worse' situations and I can't just bail out on her."

"And you won't. But she has to make the choice to heal it. You have no power over her, but you can support her."

I turn and give him a hug. "Wise words..."

He holds me tightly. "Well, maybe it'll still work out." He lets go. "I'm here if you need me."

"Thank you. You have always been there for me. Remember the two of us fighting off those bullies as kids?"

Chris raises an eyebrow. "Oh, do you remember doing any fighting?"

"Chris, you are my oldest friend. God, I met you when I was two years old. I remember when they brought you home from the hospital. In those first ten years I don't think we spent more than five minutes apart. Man, we were so tight."

I choke up and let a tear run down my cheek.

"Sorry. I guess I'm feeling emotional here in the old New England fog. It looks a lot like the end of the movie 'Casablanca.' I guess we will always have Paris."

He hugs me tightly. "Yes, we will always have Paris. You're still my best friend and you always will be." He hugs me again. "I love you, brother."

"I love you too."

Chapter 22

"The heart is a sanctuary of which
There is a little space
Wherein the Great Spirit dwells
And this is the Eye
This is the Eye of the Great Spirit
By which He sees all things
And through which we see Him.
If the heart is not pure
Great Spirit can not be seen."
Black Elk

When I return to the room, I find she has passed out, so I climb in the bed and try to sleep.

With no luck...

Perhaps she is right, and I should have left her there. I knew at the time there was a strong element of rescuing to our dynamic.

At some point in the night, I fall asleep.

As the sun creeps through a window, I silently slip out of her unconscious embrace, shower and leave to get some coffee. With java in hand, I take a long walk down Water Street. The white pristine picket fences are covered with rose bushes, and their flowers are generously filling the air with their heavenly fragrance. The morning is Vineyard-perfect, with a crisp blue sky unsoiled by a single cloud.

I walk down a seashell path past the historic lighthouse and watch as the sailboats ride a steady wind past the point and out to sea.

Fifty yards down the beach a golden Labrador implores his owner to throw an old tennis ball into the chilly harbor waters. SPLASH! The beast jumps in with gusto, retrieves, returns, shakes, throws down the prize at the man's feet, and then barks impatiently until the process is repeated.

As I watch the lab jump into the water in pursuit of his prize, part of me envies his carefree existence.

Though I am perfectly content to sit right here for the rest of the day, a realization creeps in: I need to get back and deal with my girl.

I enter the room just as the Miracle is getting out of the shower. "Good morning, Pauly. Where did you go?"

"Oh, to get some coffee, and then down to the lighthouse."

She looks out the window. "Another splendid day."

"I got a text from Jack Daniels saying, 'We are on the plane and the coast is clear.' So we can pack up and head back to the big house."

You can cut the awkwardness between us with a knife.

"Pauly, I need to get some coffee too."

She comes over and hugs me. "I'm sorry about last night. I just had way too much to drink, and I hadn't eaten all day. It hit me hard. No more for me; I'm taking a break from alcohol for the rest of the summer."

"I appreciate the apology. You said a lot of things last night that were quite vitriolic. I am going to need some time to process things."

"Don't take any of my stuff seriously. I was just smashed."

We get our things together, check out, and head back to the Great Palace of Sad People. Throughout what feels like a long day, the words are sparse between us. Near sunset, her mother calls to see if we are planning to come to the family reunion.

After they hang up I see an opening. "Why don't you go back alone and take some time there with them. I will stay in Edgartown to focus on promotion and sales. To be honest, I also think a break would be healthy. This dynamic simply is not working for me. I'm sorry."

She looks a bit surprised, then down and then into my eyes. "Do you feel it's over?"

I shake my head. "No, just pausing for perspective."

I strain to find more words. "Life is short and the summer is shorter. I need some peace to clear my head. I literally can't do another night like last night. I think that was my last crazy one. The emotional whiplash is wearing me out. We can be so close, so intimate and..."

"I'm sorry, Pauly. I'll quit. I promise."

"I know you mean it sincerely, but I don't trust it. There's a nasty pattern here and we need a break." My mouth twists at one particular memory. "Last night you said I shouldn't have brought you back."

"To the Vineyard?"

I chuckle blackly. "No. From San Diego, when we met."

"I did? I'm sorry. I definitely didn't mean it."

"Maybe. But you said it, and honestly, I think you're right. I think it was the wrong move. I really think you need to consider some kind of professional help. Granted I am not an expert in addictions or drinking binges, but this can't be normal and it's certainly not healthy."

Forty-eight hours later I'm standing at the airport watching her flight ascend through the clouds.

As the plane lifts higher, so does my mood. A huge sense of relief comes over me, like a deep exhale. Then comes a wave of sadness for the state of things, and then another.

Later, at the Parental Asylum, I share a low-key dinner with my parents, brother and his wife. With Chris's partner there, I have to adjust to a much more subdued and measured version of my brother. The Fabulous-Walk Chris is now hidden beneath the subservient partner facade.

"We are leaving tomorrow and headed back to New York City," he declares. "It's been a nice visit. Thank you all."

My brother's wife sits quietly and somewhat catatonically. Who knows? Maybe there is something about our family that shuts her down? Is she on medication? I decide to heed the wise words of Billionaire Bob and not take it personally.

After dinner I offer, "Is anyone up for a walk through town? I need to spend some of this Larry David book money, and my financial advisors tell me it's a good time to invest in ice cream."

My brother chuckles. "I'll go." He looks toward his wife. "How about you, sweetie?"

Sweetie takes a moment, and then says blankly, "No thanks, but you go."

"Chris, I'll wait outside for you." I hug my mom and dad goodnight and stand under a glorious dome of infinite stars.

A couple of minutes later he comes out. "Hey man, I think I am going to stay here with her. She's feeling under the weather and probably needs some attention. I'm sorry. Let me call you when I get back to the city."

We share a nice hug and I watch him walk away and into the house.

~~~

Two days later, I reach across a white picket fence in Edgartown to pet a handsome golden retriever. "Good dog..." His tail wags and he leans into my hand. "Good boy."

A fit man in his early sixties, with a Tom Selleck mustache and a deep tan, calls to me from the porch. "Be careful with that character. He'll make you stand there all day."

"There are worse fates. He's a lover. It makes me miss the dog I had as a kid."

"Feel free to take him! We've grown tired of his relentless demands."

I laugh. "That's all I need, another prima donna." The tail wags.

The man takes a closer look at me. "Hey, aren't you the guy who likes to hitchhike, eat pizza and wrote about it?"

"Depends on whether you like what I said."

"Well, I bought a dozen copies to give away to my friends. Does that tell you anything?"

"Then I'm your guy." I point towards the golden. "Did he read it?"

He laughs. "If you have the time, come up and grab a seat. I'd love to chat with you."

My inner voice tells me to stay open, because you never know when the magic will happen.

"Why not."

The man extends his hand. "My name is Ron. I'm pleased to meet you. Though I feel like I know you after reading your work."

151

"Thank you. I never assumed anyone would read it. Serves me right for being short-sighted. Who is this friendly character?"

"His name is Harley. Care for a little lemonade?"

"Yes, thank you." He hands me a glass. "I appreciate the kindness."

"May I ask how are your sales?"

I laugh. "Better than I ever imagined. Look at this." I take out my phone and show him a picture of three people reading the book on the fast ferry back to Manhattan. "Someone sent me this yesterday. It's crazy. I had no idea this would be happening. It's been fun, unexpected and wonderful."

"It's very well done. I think it will touch a lot of people. I hope you're writing another one."

I laugh again. "Not at the moment. And honestly, I'm not sure I could ever do it again. I think I just got lucky."

He shakes his head. "Your success has nothing to do with luck, at least in terms of the writing. I have to ask, as I'm sure everyone does: did you get back with the Miracle?"

I look into his eyes. "You did read it. Thank you. Well, we did, at least for now."

"How's it working out?"

"Honestly, it feels worse than before. We love each other, and there's a tremendous connection, but in simple terms, it just doesn't work."

He makes a face that looks like he has some bad news to deliver to someone who had a spot on their lung x-rayed. "Relationships are tough. You have to fit just right to have any chance at happiness."

I wince. "That doesn't sound promising. Are you married?"

"It will be twenty-two years in September, and she's a doll."

"Any children?"

He shakes his head slowly. "No, we honestly never felt the need to. We love kids, but don't want to be parents. It wasn't a hard choice, more of a natural one."

I take a long sip of lemonade and pet Harley. "Do you ever feel like you missed something?"

"No. Besides, I have a lot of employees, so they feel like my kids. Neither of us wanted babies, so we never chose to create one. It was fairly simple. How about you? I'm guessing no."

"Correct, Ron. I never felt led to procreate, despite a love of children. I guess I am more of a dog person." I reach over and pet the ever-wagging golden.

"Harley is happy to hear that," Ron says.

"You've been successful in your marriage. Any advice for a neophyte?"

He considers my question for a moment. "You have to come at it as equals. You can bring different strengths to the table, but basically, both of you have to be happy with who you are, and with life in general. You can't fix anyone or make another person happy. There has to be respect, trust, compatibility and a deeply shared sense of values."

"Wise words, brother! Thank you. I wish I had sat here with you about four years ago. Did you ever have to deal with a partner's alcohol issue?"

He's a straight shooter. "As in, they drink way too much and are probably an alcoholic?"

I laugh. "Definitely a better way to put it."

"Yes. My first wife was an addict. It started with alcohol, and then she got into pills later. It was a nightmare. Even after we split, it took me years to get over."

"I'm sorry if my questions are too personal."

He waves me off. "Not at all. But back to my ex. At the time, I spent a fortune on rehab facilities, but in the end nothing ever worked. It was tragic. She was a captivating woman and I loved her madly, but there was not a single thing I could do to save her. If I'd stayed, it would have destroyed both of us. I understood it intellectually—she had grown up in heinous circumstances—but emotionally, I can tell you, living with addiction can ruin your life. Are you dealing with it now?"

"Yes, sadly. And it keeps escalating. How did you get out alive?"

"To tell you the truth, I don't know." We both laugh. "I got a break when she walked out and left me for someone else. Which is eventually what they all do. Three months later, she was back at my door, but enough time had passed for me to say 'no thanks.' Though I have to admit, it was tough. Remember, I loved her."

"And then..."

"I moved... or more accurately... fled."

We look at each other and laugh again.

"Maybe not a bad idea."

He shakes his head, and in his eyes I can see that some of the pain is still raw. "For about seven years I was afraid to even date anyone, but eventually I got a huge break and met my wife. You have no idea how easy it can be when you meet the right person. But more relevant, you have to be the right person, and be ready for someone on the healthier side of the curve. Otherwise they will pass you by without a second look."

He takes a sip of his drink. "I had to take a long vigorous look at myself during those seven lonely

154

years. It gave me time to grow and figure a few things out. I was able to understand and own my choices and then make some changes. But I did, and it paid off."

"Did you ever figure out why you chose this woman?"

"That is such a complex question and answer. Not to make excuses, but I am sure part of it had to do with being in Vietnam. I spent a few years in combat and it fucked me up."

"Thanks for serving. I feel it was the wrong war, but that does not detract from brave guys like you going over there to serve."

"I wasn't brave. I got drafted. I grew up in a very small town, so going over to the jungles, with all that death and destruction, was like nothing I could have ever imagined. Of course, the whole war was built on lies, and continued on lies until the pathetic house of cards collapsed. It was just another colonial land grab. Have you ever read 'A People's History of the United States' by Howard Zinn? I believe it to be a masterpiece."

"Twice in fact. It is one of my all-time favorites. Sobering in its truth."

"Yes."

This is rapidly turning into the most interesting and compelling conversation of my summer. "What was the hardest part of being in Vietnam?"

He thinks for a moment. "Probably knowing you might die at any moment. That every second could be your last, so there was a profound immediacy to the experience. Human beings can adapt to almost anything, and after a while I did, but what a price to pay in terms of your soul. This was something profoundly damaging."

We sit for a few moments in silence before he continues.

"When I got out as a captain, I had no idea what to do. I bounced around and met this troubled woman who needed to be saved. You know, thinking about it now, I was probably recreating an element of the danger I had grown accustomed to in Vietnam."

"That's deep. You at least have the war to blame. I don't have any good excuses."

He laughs. "Love is excuse enough, my friend."

I take a deep breath and dive down into my soul. "You know, maybe I tried to save her as a way to feel like my life mattered. That if it wasn't for me, this person would not be able to make it. At the time I had no idea what my purpose in life was. Her showing up gave me a reason to get up everyday that was bigger than my own selfish interests."

He cocks his head. "That's a hell of an insight, my friend. But also remember, the heart has a will of its own and who can say why we fall in love with the people we do. Hey, if you hadn't met her, there would be no book. So it can't be a completely negative experience."

"That's true."

"If she has a drinking issue, there's nothing you can do for her unless she sees it as a problem and takes action. Otherwise, she will just grow more and more frustrated with you. The addict blames the world for their problems and usually avoids looking in the mirror at all costs. You don't need to make the mistakes I did."

"Wow. I stumbled into some wisdom today, not to mention a wonderful dog and tasty glass of lemonade."

"My wife squeezes this stuff fresh. I'm telling you, I married an angel."

I finish my drink then point to the four-legged guy lying on my feet. "I think I'm going to take you up on your offer and keep Harley."

He reaches over and pets him. "Hey buddy, do you want to go with your new friend and watch him write?" The tail keeps wagging.

"Ron, I'm almost compelled to say, 'Don't hurt him.' If you get my drift."

Captain Ron laughs out loud. "That was one of the funniest parts. Do they actually say that?"

"Every time I touch Max, yes."

We stand up and Ron shakes my hand. "Please feel free to drop by anytime. I sit on this porch every day and watch Harley work the room." He points toward their front yard.

"Ron, I appreciate your observations and wise words."

"Please come back and see us."

Chapter 23

"Two drifters, off to see the world,
There's such a lot of world to see,
We're after the same rainbow's end,
Waiting 'round the bend,
My huckleberry friend,
Moon River and me."
Johnny Mercer

Mom and I share a cup of tea in the cabin and look over some old photos. "Here you are as a young child with your brother. What a wonderful time. My two boys... And this is me holding you when you were about sixteen months old, when we lived in Miami Beach. You used to do all these pushups in the sand and the people would count."

"Mom, you look so attractive here."

She smiles. "Thank you, darling. We used to take you everywhere with us. We were all so happy. Aren't we blessed to have each other?"

"So deeply blessed. You and Dad did a phenomenal job."

"Your father is such a good man. I got so lucky when I met him, especially with all the horrific men from my family. Somebody must have been watching over me. Probably my Irish ancestors, the Druids. They were the early mystics. As Okeefes, we come from them. They were some of the first Irish kings. I've always felt a deep connection to these ancient people, almost like a piece of me is still a part of them. Remember our lovely time together in Ireland? You were so kind to take me there. And then seeing Stonehenge... my lord, that was otherworldly."

"Mysterium Bellus et Fascinans—the beautiful and fascinating mystery, the unfathomable magic of this moment." I reach across the table and gently take her wrinkled hands. "I love you, Mom."

She looks straight into my soul. "I love you... Oh, here comes the man himself." She gets up and gives my dad a hug and kiss. This is their morning ritual: taking a few slow moments to soak each other up.

Dad says, "We woke up again and get another day together." He looks out the window. "What a beauty! How are you, son? Did you sleep well?"

I get up and give him a hug and a kiss on the cheek. "I slept deeply, thank you."

He's in his old white bathrobe and slippers. "Son, do you mind taking me down to the grocery store so I can get a few things?"

"I would love to. Let me go hitch up the team."

Mom says, "He has always done all of the shopping. What a sweetheart. He takes such good care of me."

He gives her another hug. "As long as you continue to behave yourself. But if you step out of line, I'm going to put you in an old folks facility. Or, maybe I'll just go to the veterans home. I think they would take an old vet like me."

She laughs. "No you don't, and no I won't." This is a familiar exchange between them.

Dad looks at me. "Let me change and get my coupons so we can go."

We drive down to the store in my Prius. "Look Dad, no traffic at the Triangle. The gods must be with us."

"Thanks for taking me, son." He pats my leg. "I hope you don't mind my crazy coupons. You know it's hard to shake a depression era mentality. In fact, I don't think you ever do. To go hungry, to not have enough, scars you for life."

My heart breaks for him. I feel grateful this man provided abundantly for me from day one. "Heavens, no. Look at all you and Mom were able to accomplish by being smart with your money. I have only admiration for you."

After a moment I add, "I'm sorry we had our struggles last summer. I think it was my fault for being so judgmental and believing I knew better than you. Looking back, it seems ridiculous and embarrassing to have this mindset. Either way, I'm sorry."

"Don't be too hard on yourself. We are all just doing the best we can. It's behind us now. It's in the past, and I'm glad you're here now."

"Me too."

He looks out the window and then grimaces. "I don't mean to pry but is everything going along well for you and your girl?"

Dad has always been super-respectful about my life and seldom asks a probing question, so I try to give him an honest answer.

"We are struggling lately. I'm not sure it's going to work. Right now, this break feels healthy. Though it's a shame, because I love her so."

"She's very sweet." I can tell he is struggling to decide whether to express something or not. I give him the space to think but he never says anything else.

I drop him off right in front to save him some steps, and then find him inside after I park. I watch as he interacts with the different workers and some of the locals. It hits me: this is his social life, and of course he is happy to have his son to show off.

As we stand together in the checkout line to pay, an attractive young couple approaches us. "Excuse me, are you the hitchhiking author?"

"Yes, I am. Hello."

The girl turns to the guy. "I told you it was him. Hey, we love your book. We've been trading lines from it all morning."

"How crazy."

The guy smiles. "We are kind of obsessed. Wait— is this your father?"

"Yes."

Dad, who has been witnessing all of this, says, "Don't believe a word he says about me." He laughs.

The girl rolls her eyes with a grin. "Are you kidding? You are so cool." She reaches into her backpack. "Would you guys sign our book? Please?"

Dad shakes his head. "No, let him sign it; he wrote it."

They insist he sign, and so do I, so he relents. The young couple thanks us and turns to go, but then the guy turns back and says, "Oh, and don't hurt him!"

This cracks me up, but since my Dad hasn't read it, he has no idea what they are talking about.

Dad turns to me. "Don't hurt him?"

"I'll tell you later..."

When we get home, I hear Dad tell my mom in the other room, "Today I signed my very first autograph at the grocery store."

Mom says, "You did?"

"Yes. Two kids had Paul's book and recognized us. They wanted my autograph. It was so much fun."

"How sweet," she says.

Dad comes into my room and says, "Thanks for giving me your time this morning. I'm sure you're busy."

I hug him. "Are you kidding? After the countless hours you gave me as a kid? All the coaching, fishing, rides, and baseball games... it's the least I can do. I'll never be able to pay you back, but I can try."

He smiles. "You are very kind."

Chapter 24

"So fine was the morning
Except for a streak of wind here and there
That the sea and sky looked all one fabric,
As if sails were stuck high up in the sky,
Or the clouds had dropped down into the sea."
Virginia Woolf

The next morning, back up at my palatial Chilmark estate, I awaken and take a swim in the pool, make some coffee, meditate, and then take a long hike down through the woods toward the water's edge. When I reach the coast, I take in the waves gently lapping the ancient rocks that long ago found a soft place to rest in the golden sand. The air is clean and crisp, and fills my soul with hope. A few seagulls circle above me in search of breakfast.

What a gift to have such a vista within walking distance of my doorstep.

Once here, it feels odd to rattle around alone in this huge house.

Who am I? Charles Foster Kane?

So I drive over to the Chilmark Store for an egg sandwich and grab a rocker on the porch. Since I am about an hour out in front of the lunch rush, the place is quiet.

A few minutes into my breakfast an old friend approaches. "I had a feeling I might see you here."

I break out a big grin. "This happens to be one of our spots."

"One of many..."

"Larry, how are you doing?" We shake hands.

"Pretty, pretty good; played a round of golf." He looks around. "Are you alone?"

"I am."

"May I sit down?"

"Of course."

Larry grabs a rocker. "Where's your girl? My God, she's a looker." His head bobs up and down. "I am very impressed."

"She's back on the west coast at a family reunion. I hate to bring up something unpleasant, but you kind of threw me under the bus with those comments the other day."

He winces. "I did. I thought about it a couple of times and felt awful. I'm sorry." He knows I'm completely kidding and smiles. "How's the book doing?"

"Actually quite well. I'm shocked, but it's selling. Better still, some of the readers write me the most inspiring letters on how my prose affected them."

He considers this. "I'm not surprised. You did a good job. I've had some nice feedback too."

"Really? Hey, I know I said it in an e-mail, but thank you very much for being so gracious with all of this. It couldn't have happened without your kindness and generosity."

He brushes it off. "I didn't do anything. You wrote it, and we both know how tough writing can be. Now, I did pick you up, so I guess if I hadn't pulled over, none of this would have happened."

"So true. I've always depended on the kindness of strangers."

He smiles. "You and Blanche Dubois. I'm still wondering what possessed me to pull over."

I chuckle. "Perhaps we will never know."

166

He stands up. "Well, I have to move along and grab a salad. Then go see my daughters."

"Good seeing you, Mr. Larry."

"You too. Tell your father I said hello, and he should read the book." He's smiling.

"I'll see him later and pass on your directive."

He turns back. "By the way, doing any hitchhiking?" He points toward the road. "I haven't see you out there this summer."

"I've retired. There's nothing sadder than a hitchhiker past his prime still hanging around trying to catch a few stray rides."

Larry shakes his head and walks away.

After lunch I decide to make a pilgrimage back to the Parental Asylum.

Mom greets me with a hug. "I'm perturbed with you, young man," she says with a smile. "You called me Jaws. How cruel."

Dad chuckles from over in his chair. I give him a kiss on the top of his head. "Dad, I have a message for you from Larry David."

Dad looks up and smiles. "Yes, what is it?"

"He said, 'tell your father he needs to read the book.' What should I tell him?"

"Are you two still running into each other?"

"Yes. I saw him today at the Chilmark Store."

Without looking up, my dad says, "Give him my best and tell him I'm too busy watching reruns of Seinfeld to read anything."

"Touché."

Mom says, "My house is not 'Early American Cluttered.' Why are you so mean?"

"I'm sorry. I promise to remove the nasty things when it comes out as a coffee table book."

She is still smiling. "That's not funny."

I decide to jump on my bike and take a long
ride. Being based primarily up island, where the roads
are so steep and narrow, has robbed me of my daily
rides. Throughout my whole life I have found a sense of
freedom and peace on the back of a bicycle.

I cruise through Edgartown and make a right on
South Water Street. My phone rings in my pocket. I pull
over.

"Hello, Miracle girl. How are you?"

"Pauly, I miss you terribly and my family is driving
me nuts."

It is good to hear her voice. "What about the
reunion?"

"It was actually tender. I spent some time with my
grandfather whom I adore. He's always been there for
me. How are you?"

"Hanging in there. My parents are good, the
weather has been fabulous, oh... and I saw Larry again
today."

"Of course. Did you guys go for a ride?"

"Ha, ha... We should, everyone keeps asking about
a sequel. Maybe in a twist, I could pick him up this
time? Larry did ask about you..."

"Did you tell him you kicked me off the island?"

"I did, and he thought it was a good
idea. Remember I told you how smart he is..."

"You're not funny. You seem awful lackadaisical
about my being gone. Do you miss me?"

I answer honestly. "All the time. I think about you
constantly and I make mental notes of what I want to
share when we talk."

"But you hardly call..."

*My inner honest voice wants to scream, I miss you
deeply and feel heartbroken we are apart but I have no
idea how to reach you. The dynamic between us reminds*

*me of being swept out to sea at South Beach by the
riptide, helpless and hopeless.*

*Why can't we simply love and enjoy each other? We
have so much, we honestly want for nothing. So why
must we create pain? Life is tough enough without
throwing gasoline on the embers of suffering threatening
to consume us. Through the grace of God, we were given
a second chance. And now here we are, pissing it away in
paradise.*

*I don't want to go back to life without you, but I feel
your demons are driving me out of the Temple of Our
Love that I so deeply wish to dwell in.*

"Pauly, are you there? Did I lose you? Hello?"

"I was just taking a second and looking out at the
water and thinking about us. Maybe I just needed some
space to clear my head. Miracle, please don't lose me."

She's quiet for a second and then replies, "Wow,
where did that come from? Is it... Ah Pauly, don't run
away. Well, when can I come back?"

A bit cornered and confused, I punt. "Let's decide
our plans in the next few days."

She's quiet. "I'm going to go." Click.

I feel her sadness, but I feel guarded too, and
honestly have enjoyed aspects of her absence. I move
about easily with no arguing or attitudes, no drunken
fights, just a good flow and peace. Yes, I miss the golden
moments: long hugs and the loving give and take. But
all the strife over the past weeks has taken its toll on
me.

As I walk my bike up the street consumed by these
thoughts, I hear a most distinctive voice call to me.

"Oh DARLINGGGGGGG, there you are."

There is only one voice like that in all of the Milky
Way galaxy, and it belongs to the illustrious Patricia
Neal—though to the lucky ones who know her, she is

169

simply 'Patsy.' The longtime, multi-award winning star of stage and screen beckons me from my bike over to a small table and chairs sitting in front of her South Water Street home.

"Have a seat, young man." As if suddenly under the Broadway footlights, she motions overdramatically with her right hand for me to sit in the chair to her left.

I bend over and give her a kiss on the cheek. "Hello DAHHHLING." I've called her "darling" in a completely over-the-top Upper East Side, Winter-in-Palm-Beach kind of way for years. "How are you, my dear?"

"Well, I'm not sure if you heard, but I'm dying."

Without missing a beat I say. "But aren't we all?"

She smiles slightly. "Yes, of course. But I am in the process of dying."

This no-nonsense manner is one of the many things I love about her. In a world filled with unending shuck and jive, I can count on Patsy to always give it to me straight. "Shall I call someone to put a stop to it?"

She cracks a smile. "You always were amusing and quick-witted. But I AM dying. Apparently, I have some sort of dreadful disease and there is nothing they can do."

I'm not sure what to say. "If it makes any difference, you look quite engaging for someone who is dying."

"How kind of you to say." She was always quite vain. "How's your summer going? I need informing."

"It's been a wonderful couple of months."

"Are you playing the piano anywhere?" She takes a sip from a glass sitting on the small wooden table. "I used to love to come and hear your music."

"I am not playing the piano anymore for money, only for fun. Do you remember that magical night we shared a few years back at the Old Sea Shanty?"

A smile spreads slowly across her face and her eyes get a little sparkle in them. "Oh heavens, yes…"

~~~

Patsy Flashback…

"DARLINGGGGGGG."

I am sitting in her kitchen putting a spot of honey in my English tea.

Patsy's spirit remains as undeterred and buoyant as ever, even after several strokes and a wide assortment of tragedy. "Let's move over here by the windows so there is more light. I love to be in the light."

"The spotlight or the sun's light?" I ask.

"Both!" She chuckles. "How was your morning engagement?"

"It went well. I'm very lucky to share the gift of music with people up at the Harborview Hotel over brunch."

"I was thinking you should write a song about me." She is being playful, of course.

"You know, I could, but it might be hard to find enough rhymes for the word 'Neal.' Let me see… Steal, deal, wheel, feel, keel, meal, zeal…"

"You're very clever. I like that in a man."

*I glance over at her autobiography, '**As I Am,**' sitting on the table. "Now that is a sensational title for a song."*

"As I Am?"

"Yes."

"Would you like some more hot water?"

"Yes, thank you." I watch her move across the room and realize that at one point in her life this simple act

would have been considered a miracle. "Patsy, did you ever think you might not walk again?"

"Of course. When I had those strokes back in 1965 it put me into a coma. I was pregnant at the time with Lucy and it was a miracle she was born healthy." She pours me some more hot water. "It was a long road back to simply being able to talk again, let alone walk. But I had to fight on. I couldn't just give up and lie there like a vegetable for the rest of my life."

"Patsy, where does all your strength come from?"

"I guess I was born with it. I don't feel terribly strong these days. I suppose I am. Thank you for the compliment. You're very kind to come and visit me. I know I can be very difficult."

"Patsy, why don't you come see me tonight upstairs at the Sea Shanty? I'll be playing the piano and the guitar, and if you come by, I might even do some singing."

"Tonight? What time, my dear?"

"The show will commence at eight."

"Well, I have a few friends coming for dinner. Why don't I bring them by afterwards? Would that work?"

"Will you really?"

"Of course, darling." She shakes my hand. "I'll see you tonight, then."

I turn and head for the door. I stop at the edge of the kitchen and turn back. "Patsy, thank you for sharing your heart. It's deeply inspiring."

"It is? Here, take this." She hands me her book. "I want you to have it."

"Are you sure?"

"One hundred percent sure."

I wander down to the Shanty with Patsy's life rattling around in my head. "What a unique woman," I say to no one in particular. The sound check takes about ten minutes and then I just play the piano for a while,

172

losing myself in the harmonics. The view from my piano bench of the Edgartown Harbor is striking through the windows. 'As I Am' is propped up and again I think, "what a song title."

And then, it just comes...

First the melody arrives, and then the lyrics follow quickly as I scramble to take dictation on a series of cocktail napkins.

Every once in a while a song will come like this. The cosmic jukebox will bless a meager mortal like myself with a slice of melodic heaven and all I can do is gratefully ride the wave.

That night, the place is packed with friends and members of my family. The atmosphere is electric and festive. I warn the audience, "There is someone quite well known, in fact famous, who you would probably never associate with me, but she may show up tonight. So be prepared."

Privately I feel there is no way Patsy will come down here to my speck of a spectacle, but it's certainly fun to consider it. A few more songs go by, the evening humming along, when right there at the door appears the Grand Dame herself.

"Am I too late? Tell me darling, I'm not too late."

The audience spontaneously gives her a rousing ovation. She bows, and a table in front is cleared for her and her small entourage.

As the showbiz dust settles, I sit back down at the piano and look out at her. "You kept your promise."

"I kept my promise." She is smiling.

"I have a surprise for you and these wonderful people. This morning in jest, Patricia asked me why I had never written a song for her. Well, I came down here this afternoon and this piece of heaven just floated straight out of me as if it were already composed and simply

delivered to me, the humble piano player. Okay, forget the 'humble' part."

Patsy and the audience laugh.

I hold up the book. "This is her story, 'As I Am,' and it also happens to be the title of my new song." I look at her. Her eyes are open, and I can tell her heart is too. "Dearest Patsy, this one's for you."

When I finish, there is a moment of such sublime silence it crosses my mind that perhaps not a single person in the room is breathing. I see Patsy's eyes are full of tears. I feel a tear run down my own cheek and realize I am also not breathing.

Then, as if the collective feeling can no longer be contained, the audience erupts in a deafening roar. Standing, they shout and clap their approval. I'm sure it goes way beyond the song, as the moment is perfectly gift-wrapped by the universe. Perhaps they are letting this woman know they love her for overcoming so much and with such grace. She never gave up and still has not stopped.

~~~

Now, years later, I am back on Patsy's porch discussing the end of her final act.

I look into her eyes. "How are you, really?"

"Honestly darling, I'm ready to go. There's no point going on. I feel okay right now, but this is a good day. Don't ask me to prognosticate what tomorrow may bring. It's lung cancer, you know. Such a dreadful, damned, disease...But it's fine. I'm ready."

"Well, my dear, you certainly got your money's worth."

She sighs. "I have." She is silent for a little while. "Is anything interesting happening with you?"

"I have a book out."

"You do? How wonderful. What's it called?"

"*Hitchhiking with Larry David.*"

She leans in and with a stage whisper asks, "Should I know who that is?"

I have to laugh. "A guy on TV."

"I'm sure if you wrote it, I would like it." She reaches across and places a cold hand on top of mine." Will you bring me a copy and sign it?"

"Of course; first thing."

We tap into some mutual memories, a laugh, a bit of gossip, and other odds and ends. Then we just sit for a long stretch of silence, for what is there really left to say?

A voice calls from inside the home. "Mommy, dinner is ready."

I take my cue and slowly stand up. "I'll let you go. Thank you for the time." I give her a kiss on the cheek.

"It was a pleasure, young man. Now you bring me that book tomorrow."

"I will." I take a good long look into her eyes. "Goodbye, Patsy. Goodbye for now."

"I like that. Goodbye for *now*."

Later that evening, Patricia Neal takes her last breath.

A few days later I attend an emotional service where Carly Simon sings and the great Eli Wallach and many others tell lovely, engaging stories. At one point, she is even given one last, long standing ovation.

As tears run down my face, I feel so fortunate that fate arranged a final farewell chat. What a privilege. All of it: our time graciously shared together, the stories, and, of course, our last talk.

Afterward, the hospice nurse tells me Patsy spent her last evening having a fabulous dinner with her daughters and then retired to bed. She was doing fine, and then all of a sudden, she was not. She fell in and out of consciousness.

Later she awoke and told everyone she loved them all very much. Her last words were, "I've had a wonderful time."

"I've had a wonderful time."

What a remarkable ending. Bravo, Patsy. Bravo.

Chapter 25

*"Happiness does not depend on what you have
Or who you are, it solely relies on what you think."*
Buddha

A week later I am back in Chilmark at my big empty house with my feet up by the pool. As the sun makes its lazy way towards the sea, the creator cooks up some wonderful cloud formations on the divine canvas. One looks like an angel extending her wings.

Feeling hungry and alone, I take the winding drive over to nearby Menemsha Harbor.

While parking in front of the fish market, I see a familiar face smiling at me.

"Well, if it isn't the wandering Jew." I walk over to him as he opens his arms and gives me a tight hug.

I lean back and squeeze his shoulders. "The Hollywood Birdman himself! So good to see you."

Short, extremely fit, a bit on the other side of middle-age, with silver hair and a beak that makes him look like a nervous bird, the Birdman is one of a kind. He points to the sky. "Nice, yes?"

"Dramatic. I was going to sit out there on those rocks and reflect. Would you care to join me?"

He chuckles. "Still looking for answers are you?"

"The *Tao Te Ching* says, 'The further one goes, the less one knows.' Or in layman's terms, every time I think I have just a bit of it figured out, it all changes and I realize I don't know shit. "

He shakes his head and motions towards the market. "Come on. Let me buy you some dinner and we can sit and catch up. By the way, the clams this year are fabulous."

When the Birdman beckons, and he rarely does, one must seize the opportunity. We pick up some chow and perch upon a couple of old wooden lobster traps facing the water while the magnificent sky unfolds in front of us. Menemsha is a real working fishing port, so the smell of the sea surrounds us.

He goes first. "I hear you have a lady in your life this summer."

"How did you know? Did Larry tell you?"

"Word of mouth, and I've seen you two together. Is she foreign or something? One of those mail-order brides? She reminds me of a young Sophia Loren."

This cracks me up. "Yes, she came from East Timor. Actually, I met her in San Diego. She's the woman I spoke with you about last summer. We ended up getting back together."

"The troubled one? How are things going?"

"Troubled."

He laughs. "Alright kid, give me the low down."

"It's complex, of course, and no one is more right than the other, but the last six months we seem to constantly clash over the most trivial things. We also clash over big things..."

He smiles, and then eats a clam. "Try this dip. It's stellar." He hands me the container.

"You're still pretty thin. Are you still suffering from Manorexia?"

He shakes his head. "I'm surprised you remember. But yes, no matter how much I eat, I can't put on a pound."

"You know, Bird, there are a lot of people on this island who would trade metabolisms with you."

178

"You think?"

I stare across the pond as a flock of gulls circle a school of fish. "Birdman, look at the sky."

He glances up just for a moment, then back at his plate. "Fab, but get back to your girl."

I wince. "What to say…" Can I just state it plainly? "She has an alcohol issue."

He is quiet for a moment. "If I recall, you don't even drink, like not even a drop, right?"

"Yeah, I never liked it or the way it made me feel. I don't mind if others do as long as it doesn't get out of control."

He puts down his plate and wipes his mouth with a napkin. "Any kind of addiction, if it is an addiction, is a slippery slope. If she has an issue, and I trust you enough to believe she does, she will have to see it for herself and want to change. Otherwise it's hopeless and will just progress."

A couple he knows interrupts us. This married duo considers itself Chilmark royalty. He introduces us, but after a brief fake smile, the two of them engage him without ever acknowledging me.

I use them as an excuse to hog the seafood dip. At some point they bring up Al Gore's excellent new film, *'An Inconvenient Truth,'* so I jump in.

"Oh, I know Al. I was in his community-building workshop for a couple of years back in Nashville, at Fisk University."

The Birdman gives me a disapproving look, then lets them know he probably won't come by their house tonight for dinner since the two of us are dining at this moment while trying to watch the sunset, which they happen to be blocking. The faux royalty departs with much fawning to him, but without a word to me.

I hand him what's left of the ravaged dip and point at the departing couple. "It's my fault. I took a few invisible pills a couple hours ago, so they couldn't see me."

He laughs. "Don't mind them. They are only into me because they think if I come to their dinners, I might bring some of my famous friends. People like them worship celebrity. So, of course, I never bring anyone."

"You could bring me along."

"I like you too much, kid. Besides, you don't want to be with these people."

I nod. "Good point, Birdman."

"By the way, don't think I didn't notice you all over that dip. And look at you dropping Al Gore's name. You're better than that."

"Actually, I'm not better than that."

"Stop it. May I give you some feedback?"

"You know I love it when you get real with me."

"Don't blow smoke up my ass, kid..."

"I'm not. You're just allergic to compliments."

He points down. "Eat those last couple of clams; they have your name all over them."

I put my hands up. "They're yours. I'm stuffed..."

He feigns disgust. "Because you loaded up on the dip."

I laugh. "Busted. But seriously, please give me some feedback."

He seems to think for a couple moments. "I've thought about you and our conversations from last summer. You sure you want this?"

I lean in. "Honestly, I'm flattered. As long as there's no hitting or anything."

"That depends on you. Okay, first and foremost: throttle it way back. Your best stuff is way too rich, like chocolate. Hand it out in small morsels, and be selective with whom you share. You don't want to act like some enlightened water cannon. Consider your audience and proceed accordingly."

He considers me again. "The most crucial thing is to be effective. You don't need to be right or ever feel wrong. You want to be effective. If you are right but ineffective, what's the point? Figure out what you are after and allow that to happen, effectively. Also, never ever name-drop. When I talk about the environment, I don't need someone telling me they know Al Gore. It comes off as desperate. Always be private with your contacts unless it's absolutely suited to the time and conversation."

He gestures as if the faux royalty were still in front of us. "You don't need them to like or approve of you." He jabs a thumb at his own chest. "You don't need me to like you." He trades thumb for index finger and uses it on me. This time, with emphasis, he says slowly, "You need you to like you." The finger withdraws. "By the way, what you're doing here is generous listening."

"I feel you are honestly trying to help me, and these are excellent points."

"But most people can't take feedback and get immediately defensive. Remember last summer when you were pitching your television idea to anyone who picked you up hitchhiking?"

I smile. "Come on. I wasn't that bad..."

He gives me a look over his glasses.

I laugh. "Alright, I was."

"Let people come to you about the projects and things you are working on. Have you noticed I have never asked you about anything like this? Let people find their way to your passions, and thus become more invested, which also leads to being patient in terms of connecting and intimacy. Not everyone is as fast or as open as you are in terms of sharing or interacting. Be respectful of people, and let things develop over time. If it happens fast, great. But it doesn't have to happen quickly. Some of the best things take time, even sometimes a lot of time. Let it stew. Be cool with slow."

"You, my friend, are very magnanimous."

The Hollywood Birdman is on a roll. "One more thing... Always stay present in the moment. Stay in the now, and while you are there, do a lot of 'generous listening' and put yourself 'under' people. Let them be on top, and serve them. Be a servant, be low key, and act like you belong. No matter how crazy the circumstance. If you find yourself there, wherever there is, you must belong. Right? I have noticed you always seem to be in some kind of place of serious attraction, so make sure you use this power for good things, and not for selfish reasons. Make it something good for others, lift others, and they will end up lifting you."

For a few moments there is only silence and the sound of seagulls. "I'm speechless. Thank you."

"You're welcome. Now eat those clams and let's get the fuck out of here. These Menemsha mosquitos are kicking my ass."

Chapter 26

"Never love a wild thing...
If you let yourself love a wild thing
You'll end up looking at the sky
It's better to look at the sky than live there"
Breakfast At Tiffany's

A few mornings later I sit at the faded Edgartown wharf sipping my coffee and looking out across the harbor. I see a father teaching his two tiny sons how to bait a hook and fish, just like my dad did. A large white seagull stands a few feet away, hoping to split whatever fish are caught. The Chappy ferry goes back and forth in perfect time. Three small girls share some colorful candy they got, around the corner, at the same store my brother and cousins shopped forty years ago.

This is summer in Martha's Vineyard.

Water Street Wendy walks by looking as toned and fit as ever. I wave, and she comes over, gives me a hug and says, "Hey, you. How's your summer going?"

I grin and shrug. "Fabulous for the most part. You're looking good. Did you play tennis?"

"Yes, and we won. Hey, I read your book and loved it, but I have a bone to pick with you." She's smiling. "I wasn't ever avoiding your call. It was Ted who didn't call me back. Just as well, since you guys ended up hanging out anyway."

"We did, and he's a warm and generous guy."

Wendy breaks into a warm smile. "He is, and Mary is a dream."

"Angelic! And she is so grounded, with zero pretension at all. I ran into them in Nashville; it was crazy."

"I saw that in the acknowledgements section of the book; how wild. Did it really happen?"

"There were four witnesses. But I have no idea how this whole synchronicity thing works."

She looks out across the harbor. "I'm not sure any of us knows how the big picture operates." She takes a really deep breath of the sea air, holds it, and then slowly releases it. "God, what a day. And not a trace of wind."

"It never gets old being here."

Wendy smiles at me. "So let's have coffee. And even though I am a member of the Yacht Club, we don't have to talk about sailing." She winks. "The book was so funny. By the way, I suggested *Hitchhiking With Larry David* to the EYC Book Club."

"No, you didn't! You are mad at me..."

"Stop it. I did. I mean, it's a fabulous description of the island and fun. We have a large group there and it would be a captivating read. You could even come and give a talk."

"Are you trying to get me lynched, or even worse, to receive the Disapproving Glance?"

She laughs. "The what?"

"The Disapproving Glance: truly a fate worse than death. It mostly comes from the older female members who all have the exact same hair color. I call it Water Street gray. My theory is: At the commencement of summer, the club mixes up a big batch of hair dye in the kitchen and then passes it out to the ladies. It's the only way to create 100% conformity, which is essential for those people. Conform or die! I've also noticed that the more Botox one receives, the more disapproving the glance. That said, would you still like to sponsor my membership?"

She shakes her head. "This is the kind of talk that gets you in trouble. Remember, eighty percent of the people are wonderful, and a lot of them loved what you said and wrote." She gets back on her bike. "Oh, and I want you to sign my copy to 'Water Street Wendy.'"

"You have a deal."

A few minutes later, as I come out of the drug store with a bottle of water, a handsome middle-aged man stops me on the sidewalk. "You're the writer, are you not?"

"I am." We shake hands. "You look familiar."

"We were both at a fairly large dinner party on Summer Street a couple of weeks ago. I spent most of the evening talking with your Miracle. She is a delightful woman." With a definite glimmer in his eye, he adds, "But I cannot, for the life of me, imagine what she sees in you."

"Well, that makes two of us."

He smiles. "I heard you caused a social stir on the Edgartown cocktail circuit recently."

"Wow, foul news travels fast around here. Is there anything I can do to squelch all this hearsay? At this rate I will never become the Commodore of the Yacht Club."

He gets a devilish look on his face. "Speaking of which, your book is a joy. I read it and felt it was very good; in fact quite flowing and dramatic. Do you happen to be a thespian?"

"No, I'm straight."

"Very funny. But since you brought it up, are you sure you're not gay?"

"Somewhat sure. By the way, I'll take that as a compliment."

"It was certainly meant as one. There's just no way a straight man could write prose with such tenderness and feeling. I think you're gay and just haven't come out yet."

"I won't come out until after the sequel. So please, don't tell anyone."

He looks around then whispers, "Your secret's safe with me. So if I had a nickname in your book, what would it be?"

"Good question. Give me a second... How about Dandy?"

He laughs. "How fabulous! Remember, if you ever change your mind, I'd love to be your first man."

"Here's an idea worth trying."

"Go ahead..." He's smiling.

"You know how the Christian Right is always trying to pray the gay out of people?"

"Yes..."

"Well, I'm sure it also works the other way. So maybe if you started to 'pray the gay into me,' things could change."

He smiles broadly. "Look, in all seriousness, I would love to have the two of you come over for dinner."

"We would be honored. Plus, I'm always up for a free meal and it would keep me from sneaking into parties in search of free shrimp."

"Oh Lord, another starving writer. You should meet my longtime partner. He would get a kick out of you and love the Miracle."

"How long have you been together?"

He looks off, as his mouth appears to be counting. "About thirty-five years."

"Congratulations. I shake his hand. "Now that is success."

Dandy smiles. "It's also a lot of work, but certainly worthwhile in the long run. We met years ago in New York City. We were both young and from small towns. Funny how quickly the time passes. It's cliché, but it does feel like yesterday."

"Are you guys married?"

He looks more serious. "We've thought and talked about it. Someday we might. How do you feel about same-sex marriage?"

"In terms of marriage, I think gay people should have every right to suffer as much as straight folks."

He cracks up. "You're hysterical."

"But seriously: I feel love is love. All men are created equal... though my mantra would be 'all beings are created equal.' Live and let love." I point at two people across the street walking by. "They have every right to live their private life in peace, and it's none of my business. So long as no one else is harmed, I can't imagine anyone caring how love is manifested. Live and let love."

"Well, if we get married up here, you'll be invited to the wedding."

"Count me in."

~~~

My phone rings. I answer it and say, "You're up early. We just got invited to a gay wedding."

A groggy voice replies, "I never slept. Pauly, I need to come home. My parents don't want me here anymore. Don't you want me to come back?"

Yes, I miss her all the time, but not in an aching way like last summer. She exists out there like a wonderful abstract theory, yet nothing problematic I have to deal with on a daily basis. The past couple of weeks have been serene and flowing. I am taking better care of myself, with more exercise and meditation time. My sleep has been long and sound. I'm enjoying my parents, and all the positive attention from the book.

To bring her back here feels like throwing a marble into a well oiled machine and hoping for the best.

On the other hand, it's not realistic to think she is just going to stay out there on the west coast, parked in some sort of state of emotional limbo. At some point, we either have to figure this out and proceed, or unwind it once and for all. Perhaps subconsciously I was hoping to deal with this back in Nashville, post summer.

I'm definitely torn because the Vineyard is my sanctuary and I don't want to infect it with any more needless drama.

So, what to do?

"Pauly, we've been apart for three weeks. Twenty-one days is too long, and not healthy. We have to come back together and fix things. We can work it out, but there's no chance of it happening while we're living three thousand miles apart."

Everything she is saying makes a ton of sense. She's right. We have to sort things out, come together and get this thing straight. Isn't that what healthy people do every day? But what is this pit in my stomach, this aching? Is that fear or is that instinct? Is my intuition trying to tell me something important? How do I get clear? I love her. I know that. But...what is the resistance, that reluctance?

I gaze up upon the Old Whaling Church looking quite stately and serene with her tall white pillars. "Um, and when were you thinking of arriving?"

"I want to get on a plane now. Remember the good stuff, Pauly. There's a lot of it."

"There is, and I will." Why can't I pull the trigger? "Let me call you later and we will deal with all the logistics."

Throughout the day I get a series of ebullient texts about returning, and that she has found a flight and can be back by tomorrow evening.

A lovely blond woman in her forties approaches me and smiles. "We met the other night; I was with my daughter Grace."

"Yes, Lynn from Newtown. You were kind with your words."

She reaches into her purse and pulls out her copy of *HHLD*. "I've been carrying this around, hoping I would bump into you and the Miracle again. Will you sign it?"

"Oh yes, of course."

She opens the book to a specific page. "This is where you quoted Emerson. 'If the stars should appear one night in a thousand years, how would men believe and adore; and preserve for many generations the remembrance of the city of God, which had been shown! But every night come out these envoys of beauty, and light the universe with their admonishing smile.' What a beautiful passage."

I sign the page for her, and then point towards the sky. "Those celestial bodies are certainly shining tonight."

Lynn looks up and then at me. "Speaking of stars, where is your soul mate tonight?"

"She is out west visiting her family." I hand her the copy of my book back and she puts it in her purse.

"Thank you. I'm sure you miss her when she's gone."

"Sometimes." We both laugh. "Would you like to walk?"

"Yes, I'd love to."

We slowly stroll around the village, quietly, until Lynn says, "We all need some alone time. Like right now, my family is back at the hotel doing their thing. So this is mom's restoration period, at least until they start texting and asking questions." Her phone lights up as if on cue. "See."

"You've been married for a while. Any advice?"

She takes a deep breath. "What do you know about commitment?"

"Only something vague about putting a bunch of eggs into a basket..."

She smiles and shakes her head. "Funny." She takes a few steps in silence. "I think you just have to be patient and work through the hard times. It sounds overly simplistic, but the power of love really is the key. You have to stay actively loving — love is a verb — and forgive." She thinks for a moment, and then laughs. "Forgive a whole lot, forgive all the time."

"So forgive ourselves too."

She looks into my eyes. "Oh yes. That's the most critical thing. You have to start there, or you can't forgive anyone else. Just try to stay focused on the love, and be generous; keep giving and forgiving."

I put my hand on her shoulder. "Are you an angel?"

She smiles. "No, just a mom. Speaking of which I better get back to the herd. Can I give you a hug?"

I hold my hand on my heart. "Thank you, sweet Lynn. It's a date for next summer. Give my love to little Grace."

My heart feels more open. I call the Miracle. "Go ahead and get on that flight for tomorrow. We need to do some healing."

Chapter 27

"There has never been a time
When you and I have not existed,
Nor will there be a time
When we will cease to exist."
Bhagavad Gita

The next morning, acting on a tip from a friend, I approach a lovely home on one of the backstreets of Edgartown.

I tap on the door and a rather regal and elegant older woman answers my knock and looks down at me suspiciously. "Yes?"

"Hello there." I point at the house across the street. "I heard from the Williams family you sometimes rent out your guesthouse."

She considers me for a moment. "But only if I like the person."

"Well, it was nice meeting you."

She smiles. "How long do you need it?"

"No more than three weeks.

"Alone or with a partner?

"I will be joined by my loving partner."

"Is your partner a man or a woman?"

"What answer gives me the best chance at the rental?"

She laughs. "Honestly it doesn't matter, I was just curious. When do you need it?"

"Anytime, but there is no rush. She and I are currently house-sitting up in Chilmark at a fabulous place on the water."

She points at a small cottage to the left of her much larger home. "Why in the world would you want to rent this tiny place?"

"We don't feel like up-island folks. We're Edgartown people."

She leans towards me. "I know exactly what you're talking about. Edgartown is the Vineyard."

"I feel the same way. Do you like to read?"

She lights up. "That's all I do. Well, read and drink; sometimes too much of both."

I chuckle. "Here's a present for you." I pull a copy of the book out of my backpack and hand it over.

She takes it and looks at the cover. "*Hitchhiking With Larry David*." I've heard some people talking about this. In fact, someone said it is quite engaging."

"That was probably me."

She laughs again. "It might be nice to have a writer around. Thank you. Here, I'll give you my number." She writes the digits down on a piece of paper and hands it to me. "Call me in a day and I will give you my answer."

"I appreciate this. Here's my number too."

She turns and then turns back. "You look awfully familiar. Are you by chance a member of the Yacht Club?"

Uh-oh...

"No. Are you?"

"Yes, third generation."

I reach toward her. "Maybe you should give me that book back..."

She clutches *HHLD* to her chest. "No way, Indian-giver. Do you talk about the club in here?"

"I do, but remember it's a bit satirical."

"Now I have to read this straight away. Okay, then. Call me tomorrow."

I get in the car and dial the Miracle.

"Hey, good and bad news: I found us a place in town."

"Pauly, you did it. Wait, what's the downside?"

"Well I gave the landlord a copy of *HHLD* and she is a long-time member of the Yacht Club."

She laughs. "You better keep looking then. I'm about to get on the flight and will see you shortly. I can't wait; it's been way too long."

"Miracle, I love you. Travel safe."

"Ah, I love you, Pauly."

We say goodbye and I wander back to the cabin and sit in my dad's chair. This is his favorite spot, up in the loft and right in front of a large upstairs window. His seat is surrounded by half a dozen portable radios and stacks of old newspapers and magazines. The man has always been a great lover of information, news, culture, opinion, and sports.

It's the time of day when the light comes creeping perfectly through the window. I relax into his seat, pick up a pad and start scratching out a bio.

A few minutes later I hear my father come in and say to my mother, "Hello, love. I had the nicest hour down by the pond just watching the water and all the bird life. It was so peaceful I dozed off. Is our boy here?"

Our boy?

I realize he will always see me as the tiny tyke with skinned knees being chased by bullies. The kid he taught to throw a baseball and ride a bike. The kid who sat on his lap and listened in rapture to his Brooklyn stories. No matter how old I become, or what I might accomplish, I will always be 'his boy.' Our roles are eternally bound as father and son.

Dad looks up from the living room and sees me in his chair as an old time radio plays softly on the table next to me. He smiles. "Isn't that the perfect spot?"

"The best."

Dad slowly comes up the stairs and we hug. I happily relinquish the sunlit throne to the Good King.

I point toward the radio. "Is this Glenn Miller?"

"No, son, it's the Tommy Dorsey Band. Your mother and I saw him at the Copacabana years ago, when Frank Sinatra was still singing with him. In those days we went out every evening. One night we might be up in Harlem catching Duke Ellington or Ella Fitzgerald, the next we could be at Madison Square Garden watching the Knicks or Rangers play. Ah, it's cliché to say, but those truly were the days. We had so much fun."

I look at an old picture of them on the wall. "You two were magnificent."

"Your mother was a top model, and everyone thought I was in the movies, or maybe in the mob. It was a lot of fun. How's your day?"

"So far, so good. I got a call from a guy at the Wall Street Journal Radio Network asking me to do an interview regarding my Larry book shenanigans."

My Dad raises his eyebrows. "How did that happen?"

"It was a pure stroke of luck. About a month ago the Miracle and I were on the beach a few feet from this older couple. We ended up chatting. Long story short, I gave him a copy of my book and he turned out to be a reporter for the WSJ."

Dad shakes his head. "Really?"

"Pure luck. He then gave the book to his friends at CBS Radio and NPR." I put my hand on his knee. "But now the Journal wants me to send them a bio." I hold up the pad.

"Do you have one?"

"I have an old one from my entertainment days that's hopelessly out of date."

"And you've been selling a lot of copies?"

I knock on wood. "Yes, so far. With a little luck there won't be any left when we head back to Nashville."

He pats me again on the knee. "How terrific. I have to tell you, I am really proud of you. You took this thing from a vision in your head and turned it into this profound piece of literature, touching people. I'm still thinking about the letter you read from a reader the other evening over dinner. In my whole life, I have never had anyone write me a letter like that, and you're getting them all the time."

"Thank you, Dad." Part of me aches for him, even as I appreciate his generous words. "Always remember, none of this would be happening if you hadn't done so much for me. You and Mom gave me every advantage in the world to succeed. It's like you put me on third base with no outs, so the fact that I finally scored has more to do with you than me."

Ever modest, he shakes me off. "But you did all the work."

"Just the last part. There is an old-time phrase my friend Nelson used to say."

"Is he the older gentleman in Nashville who passed away last year?"

"Yes, Father. He used to say, 'I feel like a turtle on a fence post. I didn't get up here all by myself.'"

He laughs. "Wise words, though definitely not a Brooklyn phrase. Oh, speaking of great words: thank you for the books from David McCullough."

195

"You're welcome. Did you notice he signed those personally to you?"

"I did. He is too kind."

"And like you, he's an outstanding role model. Despite his prominence, David is so humble, even with two Pulitzer Prizes under his belt. I'm fortunate to have such fine and diverse examples of success. Both of you have long time marriages that are still flourishing, which to me is the ultimate form of prosperity. Not prizes, praise and what not... but people."

"Hey son, you keep writing, and maybe you will get a Pulitzer Prize."

"The only way that's going to happen is if I win one in a raffle."

He laughs. "You have the gift of humor." He changes course. "How's your girl?"

"She gets back in a couple of hours, so we'll stay up in Chilmark for the next few nights. Fortunately for us, I don't think the owners are coming this week."

"Have they been demanding or rigid this summer?"

"Not at all, and we never see them. Having the place up there has been a blessing."

He looks sad. "Well, we'll miss you around here. But I'm sure we'll see you a couple more times before you have to go."

"Only every day. I'm like one of those fungi that never go away."

He smiles again and leans in toward me. "I still think you need to figure out a way to do some stand-up comedy."

I give him a kiss and say goodbye.

As I walk down the stairs I turn back and catch him framed perfectly between the wooden beams and try to let his image melt into my being. Someday that chair will be empty of my oldest friend, leaving me with an impossible void to fill.

I suddenly remember overhearing a conversation he was having with my mother a couple of nights ago. She asked softly, "Do you think we'll come back here again next summer?"

He answered with a whisper. "I guess at this stage we have to just take it one day at a time."

She then said, "Do you think we'll ever come back here?"

"Oh yes, dear, we have to. We are to be buried here, remember? So we will always be together on the Vineyard. This will be our eternal resting place."

"Yes, my darling. Side by side."

I walk back upstairs to him, kneel down, gently hug him and give him a kiss on the cheek. "God, Dad, I love you so much. I just love you so much."

"Oh son, thank you. What is this all about?"

"Everything you ever did. And I mean everything. I'll never be able to thank you."

He smiles and puts his hand on my arms. "You keep writing and touching people. That's the best kind of thank you I can think of."

Chapter 28

"Let there be spaces in your togetherness,
And let the winds of the heavens dance between you.
Love one another but make not a bond of love:
Let it rather be a moving sea between the shores of your
souls.
Fill each other's cup but drink not from one cup."
Khalil Gibran

During the summer season, the ferry from Woods Hole to the island runs back and forth on the hour. The ship resembles a giant white arc and carries cars, trucks, bikes and people filled with hopes for a happy vacation. I have always believed something magical happens in those six miles between the real world and fantasy island. That somewhere, during the forty-five minute journey over the cold blue water, you pass through an invisible portal to a more magical place.

On the way over to the dock, I experience a sudden rush of emotions at the thought of holding the one I love. Maybe the break did us some good and we can enter a new phase of harmony. I'm also a bit nervous, because I don't want to go back into the place we were.

My phone rings.

"Pauly, where are you? I'm here."

I look at the car clock. "Did the boat arrive early?"

There is a sigh. "Yes..."

"I'm less than ten minutes away, depending on the traffic. I can't wait to see you."

"Please hurry. It's been a long day and I'm exhausted and cranky."

I find her wandering out of the steamship ferry terminal, rolling her black bag behind her. We have a long hug.

"Pauly, I can't believe you made me wait."

No, that can't be your opener after three weeks apart. Don't go there.

"I'm surprised the boat was early. That's rare. They usually run on the minute."

"Well, you could have come a few minutes sooner. It's been a very long day, and of course being with my dysfunctional family for a month doesn't put me in the best place."

I look up at the cars packed to the gills with luggage streaming off the ferry and people greeting each other warmly in the waiting area. Everyone but her appears so happy to be here. There is a lovely sea breeze blowing in off the harbor and the fragrant smell of the ocean.

"Well Miracle, you're back in paradise, so just relax and unwind. Are you hungry?"

"Not really. Let's just go home and take a swim in the pool and watch the sunset."

"Sounds good." I take her suitcase from her and role it over to the Prius.

"Pauly, I'm sorry for my bad mood."

Oh no, this feels off out of the gate and I am immediately brought back to that nagging feeling I felt before she left.

Dealing with someone who depends on the outer world to bring them joy is a heavy burden.

Stay positive, old boy!

My phone rings with a local number I don't recognize. Maybe it's the bookstore. "Hello?"

"This is your potential new landlord calling. I am more than halfway through your literary romp."

Uh-oh...

"Yes?"

"I absolutely love it! You can stay as long as you like, on one condition."

Exhaling. "I join the Yacht Club?"

"Very funny. The person you are moving in here with is the Miracle, right? I mean, reading this epic love story, you two better be together."

"Well, my fair lady, your wish shall be granted. She's sitting right next to me and is looking forward to meeting you. Thank you for providing us with a new abode. Edgartown, here we come."

"I'm looking forward to seeing you both shortly. The place is yours when you want it."

"Thank you."

I hang up and the Miracle asks, "Who called?"

"Remember the guest house in the heart of town? Well, the woman says we can have it for as long as we want."

She lights up. "Oh Pauly, how wonderful! I just want to have a nest of our own and not have to worry about those cranky people from New York coming and going."

"They're fine, and we hardly see them. I kind of feel sorry for them. There's nothing malicious towards us; it's mostly the sound of suffering."

"That's true. Hey, have you done any writing?"

"No, I'm more in sales and delivery mode. But things are always brewing."

Her mood is shifting. "I think the good news has rekindled my appetite. Let's celebrate by getting some seafood at the Menemsha Market and I'll cook it for us on the grill."

An hour later, we are eating tuna steaks on the back deck as the sun slowly sets into the sea. The temperature is perfect, and we are doing what we do best: connecting. The two of us never seem to run out of things to talk about. I put my nose to the air and inhale the sweetest fragrance of honeysuckle on the wind. "The nectar of the gods."

She takes a deep breath and lets it out slowly. "Oh my God, it's so good to be back. I forgot how healing your energy is, and how you just get me. There's no one like you, Pauly." She leans in and gives me a sweet kiss. "I missed you."

"I missed you too... and want another one of those kisses."

She shakes her head and grins. "You'll get a few more for dessert. So you missed me?"

"Deeply, but I tried not to dwell on it. Being together and having you gone is so different from being separate. This was doable because I knew you were out there having your family thing, and you would be returning. The time flew by. I feel like I just took you to the airport a couple of days ago."

She laughs. "It might have flown by for you here," She points out at the unimaginable beauty in front of us, "but it dragged for me. I'm glad I went, though. It was good to see my family and spend some time with my grandfather. He's getting so old. It's hard to see him age."

"I feel the same way about my parents. This temporal mortality thing sure seems like an awfully cruel joke on all of us. I think the jury is still out on God's omnipotence."

"Pauly, speaking of God, take a look at the moon coming up. It's huge."

She's not kidding. "It looks like one of those super moons. Boy, are we blessed. Just look at all of this." I extend my arms fully.

We linger for the next hour or so as the mosaic in front of us becomes more colorful and the temperature slowly lowers. We share stories and anecdotes as the gigantic moon begins its journey across the clear black sky. "Pauly, I'm getting sleepy. Let's go to bed."

We make love slowly and passionately, with all three weeks of abstinence obliterated in ecstasy.

After, we lay tightly in a sweaty embrace. The moon hovers outside the window, bursting with golden light, as a series of gentle sea breezes sneak through the screen, lifting the curtains and caressing us.

We look deep into each other and profess our love. It's truly a soulful experience, and I feel like I've never been this close to another human being. We are one.

All of my defenses have been removed and we are just what we are.

She starts to softly cry.

"What is it, my love?"

As we are drifting off to dreamland, she whispers, "Pauly, please don't ever send me away again."

Chapter 29

"On the tawny close grained cedar
Burning round me like fire
And all the angels of this housely heaven
Ascending through the first roof of light the sun has
made.

This is the bright home in which I live,
This is where I ask my friends to come,
This is where I want to love all the things
It has taken me so long to learn to love."
David Whyte

A week later, the Miracle and I move down to our Edgartown cottage and settle into a nice flow. In the mornings we walk to the Harborview Hotel for coffee and sit on the expansive porch watching the boats go by the lighthouse. Lunch is usually gathered from the salad bar at Morning Glory Farm, with its vibrant and fresh selections from the fields around the island. There are long bike rides, nice conversations, beach naps, and a variety of dinner adventures.

In between all of the above, we make the rounds casually restocking the outlets gracious enough to offer me a portal for my words. Every day there are wonderful, spontaneous encounters with people touched by some chapter or phrase from the book, many who offer an intimate snapshot into their own journey.

After confirming that we have moved down to Edgartown, I get a call from Jack Daniels.

Some highlights: "How could you two quit on me? You left me alone with her. You will have my blood on your hands. I knew once your book started selling and you were raking in the big bucks you would dump me like yesterday's news. Ok fuckhead, at least promise me you and gorgeous will come back and have dinner with us. And how did you get such a gal? I hate being jealous of you, you piece of shit. But if you ever need a free ride to NYC in the plane, just let me know. Seriously, it was a fun summer and your music will be missed."

Classic JD.

One cloudy afternoon I wander back over to Captain Ron's porch for his unique mix of wisdom and excellent lemonade.

Today's topic:

"Captain, why are people so obsessed with money?"

He ponders my query. "It sounds overly simple, but they think it will bring them happiness."

I feign surprise. "You mean it doesn't? You're rich; give me the inside scoop."

He sits up in his soft seat. "If you are already content with who you are, and at peace in your own skin, it may augment these feelings, but you have to be careful, because it can also isolate you. Everyone tries to cozy up to you when you are affluent."

"Am I that transparent?"

He laughs. "You could care less. That's why you're on the porch. People think wealthy individuals are holding some sort of 'secret' to becoming successful."

"Is there a secret?"

"There is no mystery to it. The same old principles of hard work, determination, and being creative still apply. But there's also a lot of luck involved — just plain old good luck — and don't let anyone tell you differently. Yes, we make our own luck, but there is a definite magic to it all. Yet even luck, like life, is mysterious. You know. You wrote all about it."

"But I don't understand it."

He shakes his head. "No one does..."

"I feel fortunate. I mean, to even exist and then have all these advantages in terms of health and what not."

He slaps the table. "Absolutely. Health is the trump card, but let's get back to luck. For instance, Larry picked you up. That was lucky. But then you worked incredibly hard to create something viable. You probably put a lot of effort into promoting it and getting the word out."

"That's true, I did..."

Ron takes a long sip of lemonade and looks off in the distance. "Then you had some lucky breaks getting your book into the hands of the right people. Can you see there is a mix to it?"

"It's definitely a combination of elements. You have to put energy into motion, and if you do, you're bound to get some good breaks."

Ron pauses. "Someone once told me luck is where hard work collides with opportunity."

I change course a bit. "Speaking of luck, have you seen that large ship in the harbor?" I point in the direction of the water.

Ron concurs. "It's impossible to miss. In fact, it's so big it has to sit outside the inner sanctum, off the coast of Chappaquiddick."

"I hear people talking about it all the time with envy and wonder. The general sense is, whoever owns such a boat would have to be extraordinary, with prodigious abilities."

The Captain asks, "Isn't this the case in our society these days? Wealth equals value. Both in the so-called free market and in regards to human beings, money is what matters. The more you have, the more you're worth. Figuratively and literally, which happens to be one of our culture's great lies."

I shake my head. "Some days I like to fantasize about earning billions of dollars and doing all kinds of charitable things around the planet. I could still live in a way that makes Caligula look like Gandhi, but man, the rest of the cash? I would blow it on empowering people. At least I think I would."

The Captain cocks his head and gives a wry little smile. "Why not? You can't take it with you. Plus, the truth is, you would get so much joy from giving it away, your actions would actually be selfish."

"Enlightened self-interest."

Ron pours another round of lemonade and takes a long sip. "God, this is good stuff. Fresh lemons are the key." He seems to have lost his train of thought. "Oh yes, my last point. You know all this consumption we are collectively involved in is non-sustainable."

"Non-sustainable... Is that a nice euphemism for human extinction?"

He smiles. "Yes, sir."

After a beat of silence, he shifts gears. "Okay, enough about the end of the world, I have a more important question: Are you writing a follow-up?"

"That's funny. Not yet. Honestly, I'm trying to figure out what I should do with my life. My girlfriend keeps imploring me to become something larger and more lucrative, but I'm completely stumped as to what that might entail. Do you have any advice?"

He thinks about this long and hard. "Give me a minute." Sweet Harley comes over and lays his golden head in my lap. Ron looks up at me intensely. "How many times this summer have we sat here on this porch and chatted?"

I think for a moment. "I don't know, maybe a half dozen?"

"Give or take, yes. We've talked about a lot of topics and covered a ton of ground."

"Your words and thoughts have been very impactful."

He smiles. "I've also enjoyed it. And not counting you, how many people do you think I talk to at this level, this deeply, in my life?"

Now it's my turn to think for a moment. Let's see, he's married, owns and runs a bunch of companies, has been around, is friendly, so he probably has a lot of friends... "I would say twenty."

"Go lower."

This surprises me. "Lower? Ten?"

"Nope. Zero. You're the only one."

"No way. You're trying to pump me up."

"I'm being 100% straight here. Zero. Okay then, now you be honest. How many people in your life do you talk with on this level?"

I try to come to some sort of number before realizing, "Too many to count."

"My point precisely. This is your gift: connecting with people. I have no idea why I trust you and tell you the things I do, but it feels right and it's easy. This is same thing that happened with Larry David or the homeless woman in your book you met at Alley's. People open up to you. It's a rare gift and there's something to it that actually helps the person doing the sharing."

"Thank you. I've never thought about it in these terms. I just love people."

"It shows. So, my friend, figure out a way to use this gift for good, make a few bucks from it to pay the rent, and I bet you'll have one hell of a life. Just make sure you kick back 10% to me when you hit it big." He winks and laughs.

"And 10% to Harley..."

He pets the golden head. "No, he'll just blow it. Seriously, I believe you're on the right path, and you need to keep writing. Maybe you can combine the two."

I put my right hand on my heart. "I feel overwhelmed with gratitude. It's going to take me a while to unravel and unwrap what you just gave me. Sophocles says, 'wisdom outweighs any wealth,' so you have given me much."

He waves me off. "More than anything, make sure you have fun in the process. Look, it's not about stuff. I've owned a bunch of big houses and private jets. Before long, you get used to a certain level of affluence, and none of it excites you.

"Right now you have everything out in front of you. It's all going to be new, fresh and exciting. Hang on to the thrill, and if this girl is the right one, hang on to her too. But if she doesn't choose to be a healthy and grateful partner, you owe it to yourself, and even to her, to cut her loose.

Life's too short and too tough on its own accord to waste any of it putting out a bunch of someone else's self-created fires. We self-create the good, the bad, the crazy and the sane."

Harley finally lifts his head out of my lap. I give him a gentle squeeze. "Good dog."

Captain Ron laughs. "Don't hurt him."

"Don't hurt him indeed. Hey, thank you."

He stands up. "This has been a win-win. These talks have got me thinking about a lot of new paradigms and perspectives." He extends his hand, but I give him a hug instead.

"Thanks Captain, and you too, Harley."

"You know where to find us. Don't you dare leave the Vineyard without saying goodbye."

I turn and salute. "Yes sir!"

Chapter 30

"We're all a little weird
And life is a little weird
And when we find someone
Whose weirdness is compatible with ours,
We join up with them
And fall into mutually satisfying weirdness
And call it love
True love"
Robert Fulghum

The Miracle and I drop by my parents for a visit and find them holding hands on the outside deck. Sixty years together and they are still going strong.

Hugs and kisses are exchanged all around before the Miracle goes in to use the bathroom. A moment later my mom asks, "So where is your sweet lady, still back on the west coast?"

Dad and I exchange glances.

What should we say?

My Dad says gently, "She's inside, love, using the restroom."

"Oh." I can see in my mother's subtle sadness she still has the capacity to understand her short-term memory is fading away. Her face falls slightly.

She looks down for a few moments and then raises her eyes to me.

Mom looks resigned. "I guess it's all slowly slipping away."

My heart sinks, but I manage to say, "Leaving only the best of you, Mom," without missing a beat. "Trust me when I say no one misses the old you. Besides, you were always a bit confused."

She bursts into laughter. "I was fiery! It's the Irish in me, and there is nothing you can do about it."

I get up and give her a kiss. "You haven't forgotten anything imperative. It's like your mind just refuses to hang on to any of the trivial stuff. In a way, it's an advantage. Are you happy?"

She smiles. "Extremely, and so grateful just to be here. It all feels like a miracle."

"So through some biological luck, you've been transformed into the Irish Buddha."

Dad laughs. "I'm glad you added the Irish part, because she still likes her glass of whiskey every evening."

Mom says, "My great-grandmother Peg, the one who raised me, had a nightly shot of whiskey right up until the day she died, and she lived to be ninety-six."

I shake my head. "Ninety-six? Maybe I need to start drinking. Speaking of miracles, here she is."

The lovely olive-skinned one comes out and gives my mom a kiss on top of her head.

Mom smiles. "Hello darling, are you having a nice summer?" Sometimes my mother sounds like a small child.

The Miracle grins. "Yes, it's been divine. I like it so much better since we moved back to Edgartown. Our

214

cottage is small, but it's all we really need. And the landlady liked our story so much, she invited us to stay on as long we want without paying rent." She shakes her head. "The power of Pauly strikes again."

"It's not me. People are just so loving and generous, we keep getting blessed."

Though it's a long shot my parents will leave the grounds of the Asylum, I ask, "Hey, before we depart this island, can we take you two to lunch?"

Dad waves us off. "You don't have to…"

But Mom says, "I want to go!"

In a nice show that chivalry still exists, he says, "Well, if my bride wants to go, we'll just have to accept your offer." Dad changes the subject. "But I want to pay. I'm not sure you've sold enough books to be so generous."

The Miracle says, "Actually, we're down to the last four boxes. They've been selling beyond our wildest expectations."

Somewhere someone is cutting some grass. I soak in the beauty of the moment and notice some broken boards on the floor of the deck. "Hey Dad, do you need a hand around here before we go?"

"Maybe you can help me take some of this porch furniture down to the basement. Oh, and thank you for picking up all those things from the hardware store for us. We appreciate the help."

Mom looks at the Miracle. "It's gotten hard for us to get around, but we make do."

We bid them farewell and decide to go for a long drive up to Aquinnah for a walk along our favorite beach.

We wind our way past the most exquisite scenery on both sides of the road and reach the far tip of the island, where we find a good parking place and set up a small camp along the towering dunes. September brings a dramatic reduction in the island's occupancy, so there's not a soul in sight. Taking advantage of this, we strip down to nothing and go for a swim.

She points off in the distance. "Pauly, look at those clouds."

I gaze off and ponder a group of gigantic white cumulus hovering over the clear water, then take a long, slow inhale of the fragrant sea air. "Good lord, how did I get so lucky to be here with you in paradise?"

"Ah, Pauly, I love you so much. The water actually feels warmer today."

"This is the best time of year for swimming, since the sea has had all summer to heat up. The island is so much more serene once the July and August madness passes. It's not mobbed, but there are still enough people around to make it interesting."

She agrees. "You get the beaches to yourself, there's no traffic, and the restaurants always have tables available. It's perfect."

"I'm telling you, paradise..."

She submerges, and then glides back up, glistening and lustrous. "Pauly, when you make some serious money, can I get my breasts done?"

"You have to be kidding. They're gorgeous." I reach over and gently caress her. "Why mess with God's perfection?"

"No, they're not. I want them to be a bit bigger, and a lot more firm, so I can wear shirts without a bra and still look hot."

"I like the idea, but seriously, you already look so eye-catching."

I silently wonder what society has done to the female psyche and self-image when even a woman this alluring has serious issues with her body? How tragic. I decide to offer some highly selfish moral support.

I wrap my arms around her. "I think you need some physical reassurance when it comes to feeling attractive. Why don't we make love on the beach again, like we did last summer?"

"But I feel so fat."

As she exits the water illuminated by the setting sun, she looks perfect to my eyes. I love her curves and voluptuous form. Give me a full-bodied goddess every time.

On the beach we dry off and cozy up to watch the sunset light show. I reach into my bag and take out a small journal.

"Let me read something I've been saving just for you...

'...But the miracle had come simply
from allowing yourself to know
that you had found it, that this time
someone walking out into the clear air

217

from far inside you had decided not to walk
past it any more; the miracle had come
at the roadside in the kneeling to drink
and the prayer you said, and the tears you shed
and the memory you held and the realization
that in this silence you no longer had to keep
your eyes and ears averted from the place
that could save you, that you had been given
the strength to let go of the thirsty dust laden
pilgrim-self that brought you here, walking
with her bent back, her bowed head
and her careful explanations...' David Whyte."

She turns back with tears in her eyes.

Chapter 31

"A soul mate's purpose is to shake you up,
Tear apart your ego a little bit,
Show you your obstacles and addictions,
Break your heart open so new light can get in,
Make you so desperate and out of control
That you have to transform your life"
Eat, Pray, Love
Elizabeth Gilbert

The next morning I get a call from an old friend who is now producing films in Los Angeles. "Pauly, your manuscript is so inspiring. I was laughing on one page and crying on the next. How did you write this, and where did it come from? I had no idea you could write."

I deadpan. "Neither did I."

We both laugh.

"I have to be in New York in a few days for business. What if I pop up to the Vineyard for a visit and we can talk about turning your masterpiece into a movie?"

Somebody pinch me.

"Are you serious? Come on up."

Mr. Producer and I met in Nashville a few years ago. I found him to be a wonderful soul. He's also a dead-ringer for the actor/director Rob Reiner. Plus, he's the rare person you can trust both personally and professionally in the entertainment industry. When I think about it, the idea of putting my baby into his hands feels copacetic.

In what seems like a blink, he is on the Vineyard and we are diving into some interesting creative conversations on how this piece might work on the screen.

Now remember, no entertainment undertaking is ever consummated without the participants first doing a large amount of fine dining. Having no choice but to submit to this time-honored tradition, we hit every fabulous restaurant on the island. Everything is going splendidly until one evening when we serendipitously join forces with a large party at a private supper club. With the champagne flowing freely and the Miracle left unattended, we end up with a situation on our hands.

I have seen the Miracle intoxicated on a multitude of occasions, but never once this inebriated. If there's an upside, and believe me I know I'm stretching the term to the max here, it does not trigger her dark, scathing evil twin persona. But holy moses, she is flat-out shit-faced.

With Mr. Producer's help, I manage to get her down the stairs to the street. From there, I slowly walk her up the main drag and over to our cottage one careful step at a time.

Once home, the poor thing spends a couple of hours bowing before the porcelain throne. Another day full of diamonds turns into a night full of rust.

Come daybreak, I wake to find her in the fetal position next to me. The room reeks of vomit, so I open the windows before softly slipping out into the MVY postcard morning.

I hop on my bike for a pleasant ride along the ocean. With the Beatles in my ear, I try to leave the cottage and my sadness behind.

After breakfast, I get a call from the Chilmark store asking for a box of my words, thus providing an excuse to grab the Prius for a scenic drive and a slice of pizza.

As I make my way up-island, I catch sight of a young man by the side of the road with his thumb out. Karma-wise, there's no way I can pass this guy. I pull over and he hops in.

"Thanks for the ride, man."

"Of course. Where are you headed?"

"The Allen Farm on the South Road. Do you know the place?"

I turn down my music. "You're in luck. I'm headed right past it." He has the look of a healthy, outdoors type: an unshaven face, old jeans, stained shirt and tattered work boots. "Do you work there?"

"Yes sir." He says politely.

I smile at him. "Heavens, don't call me sir; I feel old enough."

"No worries. I work there part-time, and I also have a full-time landscaping gig."

"I don't see many hitchhikers any more. My theory is the overly efficient bus system has kind of driven them into extinction."

He frowns. "It's kind of a bummer. I guess people are also more afraid. Though I have no idea why."

"I've been coming here my whole life and have never heard of a hateful happening. This place is safe and insulated. Years ago, there were tons of people hitching because there was no other way to get around. We could hitch at all hours and surprisingly get rides even in the middle of the night. Plus, it was a wonderful way to meet people. But I think you're the only one I have seen all summer. It kind of makes me feel nostalgic."

"Hey, speaking of hitchhiking, there's a book you need to read. Have you ever heard of a guy named Larry David?"

I look off into the distance as if I'm trying to think about the person he mentioned. Part of me is curious what this young dude is about to say, but I also brace myself in case he trashes the book. "Isn't he the person who created the *Seinfeld* show?"

The guy thinks for a few moments. "Yes, and also a show called *Curb Your Enthusiasm*."

"And he wrote a book?"

"No, not Larry David. The author, I forget his name, gets picked up here on the Vineyard by Larry. He careens around the island catching rides in search of truth. It's pretty philosophical."

I can't resist. "Is it any good?"

He thinks... for what feels like way too long.

Uh-oh.

"I liked it a lot; it's easy to read. I blew through it in one night. There are parts where you laugh your ass off. I found it through one of my housemates, who is kind of obsessed with it, quoting stuff from different passages or talking about certain parts. She really wants to meet the writer, but I'm not sure he is even up here anymore. The book is cool. You should check it out."

"Thanks, I will. Larry David, right?"

"Yes. It has a thumb on the cover; a big thumbs up. What worked for me was that the author asked the people who gave him rides excellent questions. Some of the answers were deep, some were funny, and overall it was fascinating stuff."

I steal a glance at my passenger and try to conceal a grin. "Maybe you should think of a good question for me."

"You think? Okay. Give me a second or two."

"No hurry."

"Here's one: what one thing has changed your life the most?"

"That's easy. I stopped dating models."

He cracks up. "Come on, dude."

I laugh. "Ok, let me be serious. *What one thing has changed my life the most?* Wow, good question under pressure."

"Did I go too deep?"

"No. I asked for it." I think for a couple of moments, but I already know. "Meditation. Meditation changed everything about every aspect of my life, thus changing all of me, and definitely for the better."

"How so?"

This kid is good. "It allows me to see beyond my mind, to catch fleeting glimpses of who I really am, and not the idea of me. Going within allows me to not just see a larger reality, but to feel one. My mind, with its small, limited story, is my greatest obstacle to being happy. Trust me when I say I am an awful candidate for stillness, because my thinking is so consuming, but over time and with a lot of practice, this shifted. I sleep well, the small shit bothers me less, and I feel more love and more loving."

"Very cool answer..."

"But even now, my mind resists sitting still on a daily basis."

"How come?"

"Because, in the light of awareness, the mind is shown to be an imposter; an illusion. It has a will to live, just as all living organisms do, like a virus so tiny we need to magnify it at an insane level to catch a view. The mind/ego still has a will to live."

"So is the mind evil?"

"No. But it can create evil if left untethered and untrained. I think the problem is this: the mind is a wonderful servant but a terrible master. And in the world we live in at this time, the mind is king. Thus we see insane and unprecedented levels of suffering. But you and I can create a bit of divine space inside of us which can change everything about how we move through the world."

"Man, do you teach this stuff?"

I laugh. "Hardly. Most of the time I forget. I'm still just learning like the rest of the herd. There's a compelling read called A New Earth by Eckhart Tolle you might take a look at. Like he says, it comes down to bringing presence, you know, attention, to the moment. One second at a time."

He takes out a journal from his backpack and writes down the information. "Anything else you think I might dig?"

I think for a moment..."*Illusions* by Richard Bach, *Crossing The Unknown Sea* by David Whyte, *The Power of Myth* by Joseph Campbell, and *The Prophet* by Gibran... that list should keep you busy."

"Bro, huge thanks. Are you sure you're not a teacher?"

"I'm a student like you, just older."

"Oh, shoot... there's the farm." He points to the right at a mailbox and gravel road. Appreciate the talk, man. What a ride."

I pull over and let him out. "What's the name of the one you mentioned?"

He thinks. "*Hitchhiking With Larry David*. Funny, you sound a lot like the dude who wrote it."

"Remember there are no coincidences." I hold up my hand. "Keep your thumb up."

He gives me the thumbs up as I pull out.

Now that was cool.

After dropping the books off and picking up a slice of pepperoni pie, I decide to drop in on David McCullough. This time I find the Good King in his kitchen making dinner.

"Two Pulitzer Prizes on the mantle and the man still cooks supper?"

He gives me a playful look. "I make a wonderful spaghetti sauce. Can you stick around for supper?"

"I wish, but I just ate. Let me leave you to your culinary adventures. I just wanted to say goodbye."

"Goodbye?" He puts down the stirring spoon. "When are you leaving?"

"Sometime in the next couple of days. I didn't want to miss the chance to thank you and Rosalee for all the encouragement and support."

Humble King David waves me off. "There's no need to thank me." He thinks for a minute. "Do you have time for just a couple of tunes?"

I laugh. "Of course I do. For you, anything."

"Besides, this sauce needs to simmer." A moment later we are working our way down Broadway, his voice booming out the lyrics.

Every once in a while he stops to tell me the history of a song, or the writers involved in creating it. What a captivating experience. He also tells me fascinating details from his new work about a group of Americans who went to Paris in the last century. I could listen to King David talk for hours about the things he has learned. A few songs turns into 45 minutes, and we finally pull ourselves away.

A goodbye, a handshake, a hug, and I finally get out the door. Just before I get into the Prius, I look up to see him coming out front. He motions me over.

He looks down as if there's something difficult he has to share.

He then looks up and says, "I hate to pry, but I have to ask. Are you writing?"

Huh?

I consider this deeply for a moment before I answer. "I honestly haven't given it any thought. I'm not sure I have the ability to do it twice."

His mouth looks like he just bit into a lemon.

"No, no, you need to write again. You see, to write something like you did on your first pass takes a lot of aptitude, and you can't just leave that kind of ability at the altar. You have to honor it. You have to write a second book." He lets his words sink in to me. "You are a writer, and a writer must always write."

Good Lord. "I'm beyond honored that you see me this way and would say such a thing."

"I feel strongly about this." The King offers his right hand with an open palm. "So promise me you will write number two?"

Can you imagine me saying 'no?'

I'm choked up by the generosity of this man. To have him think about pissant me in these terms, and then follow me out, when it would be so much easier to simply let me go my way. The Good King is modeling true greatness.

I take his hand and shake it firmly.

"I give you my word, and again, I'm honored."

He looks me square in the eye and firmly squeezes my hand. "Good. I look forward to it."

I think for a moment. "Now remember, you didn't make me promise it would be any damn good."

He smiles. "I'm not worried. See you next summer."

Chapter 32

"Where there is love there is life."
Gandhi

After my time with King David I am flying
high. Yet I'm surprised there is no text from a
recovering Miracle.

As I cruise down the road past the airport,
Morning Glory Farm calls to ask for another carton
of *HHLD*. This happens to be the last box and I
suddenly feel a deep sense of satisfaction pass through
my being.

Wow, I sold them all. I wrote something people are
connecting with and passing around. How fortunate am
I? Then King David cared enough to encourage me to go
further. There are so many blessings.

I suddenly feel a wave of loss. The Miracle is not
beside me in this moment. Her drinking creates so
much invisible distance and damage.

As I hand over the last box to the Farm, I also feel a
twinge of sadness. It will be time to go soon. Part of me
wishes there were a few more boxes in the back of my
car to pass around the island if only to keep me here in
heaven, that the summer would never end and none of
us would get any older.

It was all so much fun. What a shame for things to
come to closure.

When I finally get home the Miracle has moved
over to the other side of the bed.

I whisper, "Are you ok?"

"Oh my God, I feel so sick. I'm sorry."

"Text me if you need anything."

She groans and I think I see her head move?

Later, post sunset, I show up solo for another fab dinner with Mr. Producer, who asks, "Where's your girl? I made a reservation for three."

I shake my head. "She's not feeling too well right now."

"Well, she was in tough shape last night, the poor girl. Maybe she'll rally and join us for some dessert."

"If she comes out of her coma, I'll tell the attending nurses to send her over. I am surprised her malaise has lasted into the evening. Usually she gets better by the late afternoon."

"*Usually?* So this has happened before?"

His keen sense of observation surprises me. "You are insightful." I continue. "Yes, it has become quite an ongoing liability."

He looks off in the distance for a few moments as if considering his next question carefully. "Has she sought any help or treatment, or maybe gone to any meetings?"

"You're implying the person in question thinks she has a problem."

"So the answer would be no."

I take a moment. "She usually blames it on external circumstances."

He leans in. "Are you one of those circumstances?"

"When the wheel of blame lands on me, yes, she can be quite caustic. I am both savior and thief, stealing from her what might have happened in San Diego had I left her there, despite her continuous pleas to take her with me. I'm magical but also need to become more successful and make a lot more money. Did you know I could be a millionaire in a couple of months if I simply decided to be one?"

"Really? Doing what?"

228

"I was hoping you might tell me."

He laughs. "I'm sorry to laugh. It's not funny. But what does she want you to do?"

"Beats me. She won't tell me. So I'm stumped. I shouldn't make light of it, but it's the only way to stay sane at times."

He looks like he's seeing into the past. "Did you know I had a similar situation with my ex-wife? In fact, the early stages are almost identical. But if you've ever been to an Al-Anon meeting, you know they always are."

"I have been to those meetings. It's both frightening and comforting all at once."

"Alcoholism is a deplorable disease."

I bite down on my lip. "You're catching me at the end of my rope on this. The whole thing has been deeply corrosive. I love her passionately, but I'm getting spiritual whiplash between the magic and madness. I feel done, but it's not over. She's so amazing, so lovely and then..."

A busboy fills our glasses with water and takes away the extra place setting.

I continue. "Right now, it feels like a sports team playing out a season after we've been mathematically eliminated from the playoffs. Secretly, I keep hoping some day she'll just wake up, literally, and realize what's been happening and shift. Then we can live happily ever after like the characters in one of your movies."

He shakes his head. "It's never going to happen without some personal responsibility and ownership."

"Then we're doomed. She's allergic to both of those qualities."

He thinks for a moment. "I'm sorry, but sadly, without treatment, it only gets worse. Take it from me, you don't want to go down this path, particularly with children. It will break your heart." He takes his napkin off the table and puts it in his lap. "You know, and this has nothing to with us working together, but I'm here for you."

I reach across the table and shake his hand. "Thank you. You've always been an excellent friend, way beyond the scope of what we ever did on a business level. Not only do you look like a rabbi, on nights like this, you act like one.

"Whatever you do, don't try to hold it in or go it alone. That's an even tougher path. Get support."

"That's excellent advice. Look I don't want to come off as flip about any of this. I think I make these awkward little jokes to deflect myself away from the enormous pain I'm feeling around all of this. I love this woman and feel powerless to help her. When it's working, the love flows and it is a force. In those times I almost believe that things have been magically healed and we're headed for a long period of smooth sailing. Then just as suddenly we are off the rails. This experience has been a heartbreaking process."

He reaches across the table and puts his hand on mine. "I'm sorry."

"Me too, brother. Me too."

The waiter approaches. "Would you gentlemen care for a glass of wine?"

For a moment we look at each other in absolute silence, then crack up.

Mr. Producer says, "Talk about irony. I'll have a glass of white, and he never drinks anything but water, so bring him a Perrier."

The waiter jots this down. "You got it. Oh, and by the way," he says, looking at me, "did he really pick you up?"

I smile with surprise, take a moment, and reply, "Yes, he did."

The waiter grins and offers a high-five. "Wow. So cool. I loved every word of it."

I slap his hand. "Thank you."

"My brother borrowed it and won't give it back."

"I would bring you one as a gift, but I'm honestly out of them."

Mr. Producer looks a bit surprised. "You sold out?"

"Unbelievably, yes. I'd order more but we'll be leaving soon."

The waiter departs and I look across the table. "Hey man, I appreciate your listening. Your words of wisdom are helpful and I feel more peaceful about everything. At least in this moment."

"Remember, my talented friend, I'm here if you need me."

Chapter 33

"People say that what we're all seeking
Is a meaning for life
I don't think that's
What we're really seeking.
I think that what we're seeking
Is an experience of being alive
So that our life experiences
On the purely physical plane
Will have resonance with
Our own innermost being and reality,
So that we actually feel the rapture of being alive."
Joseph Campbell

The next morning I get up early and take a long walk through town. The light in September always takes on a more muted tone. The harbor grows quieter by the day, the sailboats receding like the leaves of fall. The breeze today is crisp and carries a hint of cooler days to come.

Somewhere someone is burning a fire, and the delicious smell of drifting wood smoke caresses the morning air. I stop in front of a blossoming rose bush bursting with color and fragrance and inhale deeply.

Though the moment is enchanting, my heart is heavy with the weight of what awaits me. I don't have the will or energy for another post-binge talk, replete with promises of abstinence and good will. But I feel like I have to say something, and then just let it be what it is.

I'm also saddened to leave this island. There is always so much promise on arrival. Then, in a flash, Memorial Day turns into Labor Day with reluctant ferry reservations and the journey back to another, harsher reality. I don't feel ready to go, but then I never do.

A big yellow lab, followed by an older man in a faded Red Sox cap, comes up and leans on me for a few pets. "Quite a morning," the man says in a thick New England accent.

I break into a big grin. "It sure is. This guy is awfully friendly."

He smiles. "Yes, he is quite the lover. Enjoy your day, my friend."

The healing vibrations of the Vineyard allow us to be open and relaxed with each other. I will always be a small town boy at my core. Yes, I can play the big city game, quite well in fact, but my soul lies in the heartland experience and its deep sense of shared community and fellowship.

I get a text.

"Pauly, where are you? I just woke up and there is no note. I miss you."

I text back, "Walking through town. Can I bring you a latte?"

"Yes, please. Love you!"

I bring her the coffee and a freshly-baked muffin. With puffy eyes, she doesn't look so hot.

"This coffee tastes delicious. Thank you. I must have slept for twenty-four hours. Maybe I needed it. What did you do last night?"

"I had a wonderful dinner with Mr. Producer. He's leaving this morning and going back to Los Angeles. I think I'm going to give him an option on the film rights. He's a good soul."

"Pauly, another victory." She takes a sip of coffee. "I'm sorry I was out of commission yesterday."

"I'm sorry too, love."

She looks up with such sadness in her eyes.

I sit down closely in front of her, take the coffee from her hand and put it on the table, then take her hands and look into her eyes.

"I can't live like this. I can't do it. It's too soul crushing. I feel helpless to help you."

She seems stunned for a moment and then breaks into sobs. She covers her face and weeps.

I hold her and cry too.

"I'm so sorry..." She repeats between her tears.

She gets up, goes into the bedroom, and closes the door behind her.

I follow her in, but she says, "I just need some time alone, please. I'm going to take a shower. I'm sorry, Pauly; I don't know what's wrong with me."

Reluctantly, I leave her alone.

My feelings are all over the place. There is a profound sense of loss and sadness mixed in with a pervading powerlessness. If anything, saying 'enough' gives me a small semblance of activating my personal power. Still, I feel deeply concerned for my best friend and lover.

I leave for a long drive and she decides to take a jog along the winding county road.

In the late afternoon, we both arrive back at the cottage and she suggests a bike ride over to the beach for a talk. "Pauly, I always feel clearer there."

When we arrive, the sea is like glass, serene and endless. There is no way to look at this vista and not feel a sense of personal expansion.

"Pauly, I have an idea. We have the place for as long as we want it. The Vineyard is so restorative, why don't we stay another week and just make it our honeymoon? I swear to you I won't drink another drop here. We can relax, ride the bikes, go to the beach, dine out, visit your parents, take long walks, make love every day, and just remember who we are together. I don't want to leave this place with a bitter taste in our mouths. The Vineyard is ethereal; we can't let any madness ruin it."

I watch the water tenderly kiss the shore and think about it. There's no real compelling reason to exit nirvana. I mean, where are we going? Nashville will be there when we get back. On the other hand, I wonder what will be different? I feel done, but how can I rebut such an earnest offer to simply enjoy a few last days?

I'm also skeptical that anything deep or profound will change, but the romantic in me longs for a happy ending to the summer. She is trying and reaching toward me. What if I say no and this was the one chance she needed? Who else does she have? Maybe this is about her and not me and I have to be willing to be vulnerable one more time? Heavens, the woman I love is asking for a week.

"Let me be honest with you. I feel very cautious. But I appreciate your caring enough to not just give up, so I will meet you halfway and say yes."

She holds me as tightly as possible and whispers, "I so love you."

"Miracle, I would also like to use this time to try to unravel some of these patterns with us so we can transcend our dysfunction and go deeper."

She is still holding me tightly. "Absolutely. Pauly, I won't let you down. We'll find our magic once again. I promise."

In a pleasant surprise, the Miracle and I enjoy a wonderful summer coda over the next seven long, glorious days. The weather is warm, and most of the time there's not a single passing cloud. We keep it simple.

When left undisturbed, love flourishes.

One brilliant day in Aquinnah we lay in each other's arms. She whispers, "Pauly, thank you for this week, this chance. We needed this."

"Sweet pea, it was you who led us, and it was an excellent choice. The Vineyard will always be a light on our horizon."

She sits up and looks off in the distance.

"Miracle, what is it?"

"I was just thinking that you did it. You decided to write and you did it. Just stop and think about how incredible that is." She leans back down and her soft lips kiss my cheek. "You did it, Pauly. I'm so proud of you. My sweet magical man."

"That means so much to me that you say that. You've really been in my corner on this book."

"You will always have *Hitchhiking With Larry David* as something you created and gave to the world."

I smile at the thought. "Yes, I will." There is a long, still quiet time between us, punctuated by the sound of the gentle surf touching the edge of the ancient sands. I watch an osprey survey the shallow green waters for a potential meal as a couple of seagulls effortlessly float by riding a silent tailwind. She touches my hand and sweetly asks, "When you look at such beauty, what thoughts do you have?"

I take a long, deep breath. "The kingdom of God is spread amongst the earth, yet man does not see it."

"How moving. Did you come up with those words?"

"No, my dear, it's a quote from Jesus in the Gospel of Thomas."

Chapter 34

"There are only two ways to live your life.
One is as though nothing is a miracle.
The other is as though everything is a miracle."
Albert Einstein

The Vineyard gifts us with a gorgeous last day of endless blue skies replete with streaks of white billowing clouds. We ride our bikes around town in the morning, and then pick up my parents out at the Asylum for lunch at the Atlantic Cafe.

Though located only two miles from the cabin, this is their first trip all summer into downtown Edgartown. As we pass through town, they soak it up like two children seeing it for the first time.

"Wow, look at the Whaling Church and all the sailboats!" Mom exclaims.

Thanks to our friend Jaime, the owner of the Atlantic, we once again sit at a lovely table right on the water. A moment later, courtesy of the man himself, a nice bottle of wine arrives. I feel my stomach tighten with sudden anxiety, but to my surprise, the Miracle abstains.

We all fill ourselves with fresh seafood and goodwill.

Jaime comes over to the table. "In your fabulous book, you told the world how wonderful my place is, so now we're getting a lot more people coming in to experience our fine establishment. As a small way to say thank you, your lunch today is on me."

Good karma abounds.

After dining, we give my parents a mini-tour around the village, and then drive them home for a difficult farewell.

Mom and I shed tears. Dad holds on to me for a long time, and the Miracle tears up. Promises are made to see each other as soon as possible. Then Dad slips something into my hand. It's a check for $1000. "Dad, how generous. What's this for?"

"Traveling money, or whatever you want to do with it. I'm proud of you, son. You've accomplished something magical."

I take a deep look into my father's eyes. "We've come a long way from last summer, Dad. I can't tell you how much that means to me. Thank you."

He offers a gentle smile. "Sometimes an old dog can learn a few new tricks if he gets a chance and a little lucky." He gives me a firm hug and then embraces the Miracle. "You two drive safely and let us know when you make it back to Nashville. Maybe we'll see you again over the holidays."

Mom joins in and hugs everyone too. With tears coming down from her eyes, she stammers, "I'm sorry I always get emotional. It seems more so with every passing year. We never know which goodbye will be our last."

It is a fond farewell and I ponder how long I've known and loved these two beings. God, where did the time go? When did they get so old? Will I see them again? All I can do is embrace them just a little tighter and a moment or two longer before letting go. "Goodbye."

We drive off as I see them waving to us in the rearview mirror. I say to the Miracle, "The older I get, the harder this becomes."

"They adore you. Your mom is right. Each farewell is more challenging because our time is growing shorter and we never know when we may not see each other again."

"So true, my love."

An hour later, we are driving onto the ferry for the forty-five minute excursion back to the real world. Leaving the Vineyard has never been easy, and only feels tougher with each passing season. Thank God I have the Miracle to hold on to.

We stand against the guardrail and watch as the Vineyard slowly diminishes in the distance. I consider all the highs and lows, the joy and tears, the laughter and frustration, the many moments involving the book, the people we met, the lessons learned, and the healing with my father. I turn to her. "What a summer."

"God, it went by so fast." She says. "Now what?"

"That's the big question. Well, we have a couple of days to talk about it in the car on the way home. Right now let's just enjoy this short time on the water."

She gives me a big hug. "Look, there's a sign." She points to the guy standing on the deck in front of us wearing a tee shirt with the word 'Nashville' on it.

I smile. "I guess it is."

Chapter 35

"It seems that we have been born only to consume and to consume, and when we can no longer consume, we have a feeling of frustration, and we suffer from poverty, and we are auto-marginalized."
President José Mujica of Uruguay

The miles and hours stretch out before us as we wind our way south to Music City. At some point, we playfully contemplate what we would do if the literary rights to *HHLD* suddenly sold for $100,000.

"Pauly, since you wrote it, you go first."

"Are we going to spend all of it, or only some it?"

She thinks for a moment. "What do you think?"

"I would say some of it, since we wouldn't want to be broke afterward."

"True."

There isn't any 'thing' I need, so my mind drifts around the gamut of possibilities. "Miracle, if I remember correctly, you've never been to Europe."

She shakes her head. "No, not yet."

"Then we would buy two one-way tickets to London. Let's start there and travel through the United Kingdom before catching the ferry over to Ireland. There we would wander down the west coast of the Emerald Isle, take in the dramatic landscapes, and roam the Dingle Peninsula and The Ring of Kerry."

"Then we would head to France and pick up a couple open-ended rail passes so we could gallivant around the continent. We could spend our days crisscrossing the land, staying in small pensiones and eating a variety of exotic food, all the while making passionate love in equally exotic places. As winter approached, we would wind south to the Greek islands for the warm, welcoming turquoise water."

She reaches over and squeezes my hand. "I love it; keep going."

"Of course, this would be just the first chapter in our ongoing exploration of spiritual wanderlust as we accumulate wisdom and truth through our experiences."

I continue. "Once in Greece, we would rent a cozy place overlooking the sea for the winter. We would swim naked, lie in the sun, and in the evening eat fresh seafood. In between our cuddling and naps, I would keep my promise to King David and write my next book."

"About what, Pauly?"

I laugh. "All of our wonderful travels."

She gives me a kiss on the cheek.

"Now it's your turn. What would you do with our new found booty?"

She thinks for a moment. "Well, I've always wanted this Louis Vuitton purse. It's quite handsome and elegant. I would definitely buy a Louis."

Unfamiliar with this item, I inquire, "A what? How much does that cost?"

"Oh Pauly, it's a purse. I think it costs around five thousand dollars or maybe six."

"There's no way a purse costs six thousand dollars."

She laughs. "Are you kidding? They have some that are forty thousand. The price for a Chanel purse is even higher."

Wait, for a purse?

Part of me wonders if she's teasing me. "But the purse you have now is lovely and works perfectly."

She dismisses me. "It's not a Louis Vuitton, though, or a Chanel."

Don't judge...

But I'm already there.

"You'd rather have a purse than three months in Greece swimming naked and eating fresh calamari?"

"Definitely. But why not have both?"

I consider her question. "Well, I don't think you'd need an elegant, overpriced purse on a remote island."

"But I would want one in Beverly Hills." She makes a sad face. "You know this is a sticky issue for us. If you end up making boatloads of money, and I know you will, why can't I have the finer things in life?"

It's a fair question. "Depends how you define things. Maybe they're not material."

She keeps pushing. "But how much wealth would we need for you to feel okay about me buying a Chanel pocketbook for fifty grand, or a diamond watch costing a hundred grand?"

My mind starts spinning with these numbers.

"Pauly, if we have fifty million dollars, what does it matter?" She leans in and gives me a sweet kiss on my cheek. "Don't you want me to look super hot for you?"

"Absolutely! That's why I prefer you swimming next to me in Mykonos in only your birthday suit."

"Seriously though, if we are wealthy, can't I have nice things? Isn't that a form of abundance?"

"These are excellent questions, and I see where you are coming from. Give me a moment here to ponder this." Why do I feel so confused? She sounds completely logical.

What does it matter if you have a lot?

245

"Pauly, what if you were worth one hundred million dollars?"

I'm still thinking... "I guess... I don't see any real value in designer things. Having a nice home, a working farm with solar panels, maybe an inspiring piece of art, those feel worthwhile because they serve a purpose. Wouldn't you rather take $100,000 and change someone's life forever, or maybe five people's lives?

She asks, "Why can't we do both?" Another good point...

I squirm a little in the seat. "Trust me, it's not like I want to deny you anything, but I would be lying if I said I felt good about a $50,000 purse... a purse, for God's sake! Or spending a ton of money for a watch... I want to live in a way where I never have to even think about time. The only reason for wearing that item would be to impress the kind of people who care about such things. It's simply a status symbol and has nothing to do with knowing what time it is."

I dial it up a notch. "This culture has brainwashed everyone into thinking accumulation is a sign of success, when all this collective hoarding might be the heart of what ails us. Talk about killing the flow!"

The Miracle makes a point. "I don't want to live like paupers if we have a lot. That feels like new age baloney."

"I agree there's no virtue in poverty. That's a different kind of misconception. What if we had a couple oceanfront homes to share with other people as well as enjoy ourselves? But I wouldn't want an endless array of empty rooms to impress people I don't respect. Besides, I would be petrified your family might move in and never leave."

She bursts out laughing. "You caught me off guard with that wisecrack. But Pauly, you're raining on my desires."

"I'm sorry. What you want is not wrong, or what I want, right. We just have different value systems, which could lead to conflict. In fact, it already has. I guess the bigger question is how do couples with different value systems coexist?"

She smiles. "The answer is easy: the wife is always right."

I laugh. "I'm learning that might be the answer to EVERY question."

She playfully pats my head like I'm a puppy. "You see, Pauly? With a little training there's still hope for you."

My phone pings with a text. "Peter says he's looking forward to seeing us." Something in me clicks. "Hey, think about Steve Jobs."

"The Apple computer founder?" She asks.

"Yes. The poor guy has been teetering on the edge of death."

"How come?"

"He has cancer and maybe his billions in the bank can do him a bit of good but let's just say he dies tomorrow with over eight billion dollars in cash. Literally a ton of unused and, unfortunately for Steve, non-transferable earth coupons."

I glance over at her. She looks a little impatient with me. "Keep going..."

"Now, even poor Steve realizes his earth coupons can't do him a bit of good in iHeaven. This is in no way a criticism of what he created: better, faster, sleeker, cooler gadgets. Sure, they were made in China, at huge environmental costs, but these gizmos," I hold up my iPhone, "are REALLY cool."

She takes my phone. "Yes, he created something special."

"Definitely," I agree. "But eight billion is a lot of unused bread. And think about how many people the iFool could have fed with just a part of his iTreasure? What if Steve said, 'Fuck, I'm going to keep a billion for my family and myself. I'll always have any and everything I want.'"

She smiles and adds, "And more importantly, his wife could have everything she wants."

"Exactly. They would never go a single day wanting for anything on the material plane. Never, ever, ever... He could be a hedonistic prick and do whatever the hell he wants for what time he had left and not give a damn what anyone thinks or says."

She touches my hand. "Who could argue with him?"

"Absolutely. No one could. And what if he then said, 'Now, with the other seven billion dollars, I am going to be as creative and compelling as I was selling these sleek gadgets. Just watch me kick ass as I dramatically change the world. I wonder how many people I can feed, cloth, shelter, vaccinate, educate, and assist?'"

She looks quite serious. "Probably millions and millions of human beings."

"Maybe billions. What if he founded a revolutionary iAcademy teaching people to think and behave differently, with a formula easily replicated on a very large scale? What if the iAcademy focused on peace and non-violent conflict resolution and became the standard bearer for solving challenging geo-political crises without anyone firing a shot or launching a missile?

I take a long breath, gather my thoughts, and keep going. "What if he then threw his weight behind a more efficient form of renewable energy and financed a new solar cell that gathers photons at ten times the current rate? Or if he simply used the existing technologies to create a two billion dollar clean energy project? Think of all the jobs, no pun intended, he would produce."

"Pauly, I honestly think you've had too much espresso."

I laugh. "Yes I have, but I am on an iRoll."

"Pauly!"

"What if Steve set up a five billion dollar small business iBank to fund entrepreneurs and jump-start their innovative ideas? Sure there would be some busts, but what about the ones that worked? What kind of iFuture would these new ideas manifest?"

"Is he out of money yet?" She wonders.

"No. Remember, the iFool still has a billion dollars to do whatever he wants with. Hell, if he invested it at five percent (You can get a favorable rate when you have a billion dollars), he would have fifty million a year to play with and never touch his principal. This gives him almost a million dollars a week to live off while aggressively using the remainder of his earth coupons to make a monumental difference."

"Bill Gates is making a huge difference." She adds.

"Precisely my point—and consider the influence the iFool would have on other billionaires around the world in terms of shifting their focus, from the hoarding of earth coupons, to using their wealth to actively make profound changes in real people's lives?"

"But here's the most important question."

"Yes?"

"Can I still get my Louis Vuitton purse?"

I have to smile. "Of course you can."

"I can?"

"Yes, honey, as soon as Steve Jobs sees the light."

She playfully slaps me. "So not funny, Pauly."

"I have one more thing to say."

She puts her hands to her ears. "No, I can't take any more." She smiles. "Ok, what is it?"

"Keep an eye out for the next rest area with a bathroom. I have to take a serious iPee."

Chapter 36

"Hey, don't worry so much.
Cause in the end
None of us have very long on this earth.
Life is fleeting.
If you're ever distressed,
Cast your eyes to the summer sky
And the stars that are strung
Across the velvety night
And when a shooting star streaks
Through the blackness turning night into day,
Make a wish. Think of me.
Make your life spectacular."
Dead Poets Society

Home sweet home. "Welcome back to Nashville, my dear friends." A smiling Peter Pan warmly greets us with arms wide open.

"My God, I missed you guys. This place was just too cold and quiet for my taste."

This surprises me a bit. "I thought you would enjoy some space."

He shakes his head. "No, it was unpleasant."

After unpacking and a couple of showers we settle in around the dining room table, where PP delivers some big news.

"Well, I've decided to move to Mexico for the winter and hang around on the beach with my two brothers. They have a place in a small town by the ocean. Nashville just isn't cutting it for me, and I feel like I need to shake things up."

The Miracle gives him a hug. "Good for you. When will you leave?"

"I will fly to Detroit to produce the NFL halftime show over the Thanksgiving holiday, return here for a week, then head south across the border."

I'm happy for him, but sad for me. "Abandon ship, abandon ship... can she and I come with you?"

He perks up. "Of course you can. I'm not sure how long I'll be down there, but I know I will stay at least six months. Come on down. We'd have a blast."

I turn to the Miracle. "Would you like to go to Mexico?"

She smiles. "We have to figure out what we are going to do now, Pauly."

Peter Pan shakes his head. "What are you guys going to do?"

I look at him. "We were hoping you would tell us."

"Hey, but you made some money selling your work. How cool was it to get such a positive reaction? I knew you had something special, and you proved it. By the way, I appreciated all the updates."

"Thank you, Peter. I had no expectations, so everything that happened was a bonus."

The Miracle says, "I told you guys the book was destined for greatness."

I give her a kiss. "You did, sweet thing."

Over the next few days, the Miracle and I settle back in while catching up on odds and ends. Sadly, she starts suffering from powerful, debilitating headaches that leave her bedridden.

When she takes pills for some relief, they leave her high as a kite. After a couple weeks, she also takes to having a glass of wine in the evenings, sometimes two, but never gets completely blasted or overtly hostile. If anything it makes her warmer, more relaxed, and amorous.

In the meantime, I take long walks in search of some kind of divine direction, but my calls to the Spiritual Home Office for assistance remain unreturned.

Feeling adrift, I return to my spiritual sage Saint Bonnie for sanctuary.

The Saint sits across from me and looks into my eyes.

"Oh my son, your heart appears to be heavy."

I sit in silence for a few moments. "I love her so much, but I get this strange feeling we are once again coming to a point of conclusion, and there's nothing I can do about it. There is no conflict or anything, but this still, small voice keeps whispering to me to pay attention to these last days."

The Saint sighs. "You love her."

"I love her deeply. If there was something I could do to help her feel better, be happier, I don't know. Something... anything..."

Bonnie looks into my eyes. "What can one do for another in terms of his or her life's work? Each of us controls our own path. You can offer love, encouragement, inspiration and support, but all the heavy lifting can only be undertaken by her."

I search for answers. "There is a Joseph Campbell quote about slaying your inner dragons: 'If you have someone who can help you, that's fine. But, ultimately, the last deed has to be done by oneself.' The last mile in the darkness is up to us to walk."

The Saint looks at me deeply. "Well said. Has the drinking continued?"

I wince a bit. "It got really bad this summer, then stopped for a while and now it appears to be slowly creeping back into the picture. Nothing drastic, just a glass of wine at night, but you can understand that I am little gun-shy. Oh, and now there are prescription pills in the mix."

She looks alarmed. "That combination can be fatal."

"She takes them for these bad headaches that are plaguing her. The poor thing, she can't seem to catch a break. What can I do?"

She shakes her head. "She's a sweet soul and such a sensitive person."

I look out the window, then back at Bonnie. "She always feels ashamed of herself."

Bonnie looks at me very intensely. "This is a form of toxic shame."

"Shame as in guilt?"

She shakes her head. "No, they are quite different. Guilt is something we feel when we do something dissonant with who we are. Our awareness, our conscience, lets us know we have missed the

254

mark. The original definition of sin was 'missing the mark.'"

"And shame?"

"Shame is the feeling that something within us is inherently defective, and there's nothing we can do about it. The feeling of toxic shame is unrelated to our actions, though it can cause us to act out in dysfunctional, often self-destructive, harmful ways. This condition is very common for someone raised in a fundamentally religious environment."

"You know, looking back, the irony is that I found her like this. I didn't know it at the time, but when we met she was struggling with drinking, pills, and self-destructive behaviors. But in the moment we met, she dropped all of those behaviors."

Saint Bonnie sits there listening to me.

I laugh. "She said I was heaven-sent and that I had healed her with my love and presence. She often expressed that I had literally saved her life and converted her into a beam of shining light. I guess there was a shelf life on our little miracle."

Bonnie offers, "One has to transform organically from within, or it will never last."

"So true. When we broke up last summer she went right back to the old behavior patterns; nothing had changed. Looking back, I can see where she conformed her personality to what I needed her to be, to fit into my lifestyle and my projection. But it didn't last, and ultimately only bred resentment."

Bonnie shares, "The interesting thing with addictions is the addict can have a period of sobriety, but once they re-engage in the substance, they pick up exactly where they left off. In fact, they usually accelerate their destructive behaviors, almost as if to make up for lost time. Remember, you can never save anyone."

"Didn't you save me?"

She smiles warmly. "No, my son. I just helped you save you."

Bonnie folds her hands across her lap. "I suggested books that you made the choice to read. I encouraged you to meditate and you really stuck with it."

I laugh lightly. "There were many starts and stops."

"Yet you kept coming back even when it was difficult. It was and is a series of choices that you continue to make. Never perfectly, but that's what being human is all about. Simply doing the best you can as often as possible."

"Thank you for saying all of that. I never really considered it quite that way. Bonnie, I love her, but ... but I don't want to live like this."

Bonnie sighs. "Well, my dear son, you don't have to."

Chapter 37

"And when October goes
The same old dream appears
And you are in my arms
To share the happy years
I turn my head away
To hide the helpless tears
Oh, how I hate to see October go"
Johnny Mercer

What is this haunting feeling within me that senses our days together are dwindling down to a precious few? I don't want this to be our truth.

In the meantime I find myself waking up and watching her sleep or move about the place unaware of my attention. My heart is trying to absorb the essence of her.

These moments must be savored to treasure later when she's gone. At some point they will be all I have left. In the meantime, I try to be as patient and kind with her as possible, with mixed results.

One evening we get into a ridiculous argument over what I should wear during an interview on the radio.

"They will only hear my voice. Trust me, I can wear a pair of jeans and a sweater."

"Pauly, you need a pair of slacks and a nice shirt with a collar."

I end up wearing what I want and feel vindicated when the host has on the same exact attire. When I jokingly point this out, she gets upset and leaves the room. Though extremely disruptive, I somehow manage to present a light-hearted interview.

The next morning, amidst the unspoken tension, I approach her, give her a hug, and look deeply into her eyes.

"Love, sweet love... this has to stop. We can't go on like this. We are constantly at loggerheads over the most trivial of things. Don't you see we already have everything anyone could ever want and truly need? We have each other, and we have this ineffable connection. We have the blessing that comes from something higher and wiser than us. It's a rare and precious gift. It would be a crime to piss all over it and then toss it away."

I hug her again. "To simply have the kindness of another, and the loving touch of a partner is priceless. All we need is each other, a roof over our heads, and our coffee machine."

I think for a moment or two. "Do you realize most people in the world don't have running water or will ever enjoy a single shower? We could live in a place the size of this room, dine on organic food, and read each other the finest literature ever written. We could take long walks and make love during rainstorms. Please come back to me. Let's stop all of this ego, this craziness, this madness, and return to each other fully. I don't want to be right, and I don't want you to feel wrong. I just want us to be happy together. Please hear me. This is my last grasp for you."

Sadly, she is intractable. My plea falls on deaf ears and dead eyes.

As unhappy as she seems to be with me, I'm shocked when she suddenly says, "Pauly, we need to get engaged and set a date. We need to make a commitment and stick it out, more than ever during the hard times. This is what love is, the good and the bad. Let's dive in and get married."

I listen intensely. "Yes, commitment is essential."

But in my heart I feel this would be disastrous. What would a ceremony or a piece of paper accomplish? How would this heal the deep mortal wounds that haunt us? As much as I love her, I can't imagine living the rest of my life in this type of madness. I don't want the presence of alcohol and chemicals darkening my existence.

I feel more authentically myself and truly free to be me when she's not around. Granted it is always more comfortable to be solo, but there has to be a middle ground, a balance, that's healthy.

Yet even as we move through these death spiral days, there are moments of blinding beauty. Of laughter or epiphany, or some shared something that transcends all of our ego-related bullshit.

I think about the last days of the Beatles. How even in their final most lugubrious months, the Fab Four created a masterpiece in the album, Abbey Road. Maybe she and I are like members of a band that make the most spellbinding music, but eventually break up because they simply cannot get along.

From dissonance and pain come art, fierce beauty and rebirth.

Being a hopeless optimist, I still keep thinking one moment she will simply wake up and 'get it.' But a few nights later, my hope takes a major hit. Literally.

After a nice warm shower, I go into the closet to pick out a tee shirt before bed. When I bend over to pick up a fallen hanger, I suddenly feel a vicious slap across my naked ass.

"Oh my God, that really hurt!" I turn to see her grinning behind me and look in the mirror where a huge red mark is immediately swelling. "Girl, what the hell were you thinking?"

She giggles. "Oops, I guess I hit you too hard." More giggles. "I'm sorry. Hey, but the bruise even looks like a hand."

My ass hurts, so I go to get some ice. "What the fuck?"

She immediately turns dark and belligerent. "Don't yell at me. I was only joking." It's apparent she's taken a pill and maybe had a glass of wine. Or even worse, it looks like the evil twin has shown up, obviously aroused from the dark inner dungeon in which she abides, patiently waiting for the right amount of alcohol, and now pills, to escape into the moment and wreak havoc upon those she professes to love most.

She gets up close to me and sticks out her chin saying, "Do you want to hit me back? You want to get even? I bet you do..."

I realize she *really* does want me to hit her.

I back away and sit on the bed. "Is this what happened when your ex-husband hit you? Did you hit him first?"

The question seems to throw her. "Well, we were fighting and maybe he grabbed my arm. Then I slapped him across the face, and he punched me so hard, it knocked me out."

"Were you drinking that night?"

"We'd been at a bar, drinking, yes. So what? He should never have hit me. He knocked out two of my teeth."

"No, he should not." I stand up and look again at the bruise. "It hurts, but the ice is helping."

She gets a sad face. "I'm sorry I hit you. I didn't mean it. Can I make it up to you?"

"No, not tonight. We can talk about it tomorrow when you're clear."

"I'm totally clear. Let's talk tonight. It was just an accident. You've slapped my ass before."

"Playfully maybe, but never like that."

I throw the ice in the sink, turn out the light, and jump into bed.

She gets in next to me and, in the darkness, asks, "Aren't you going to make love to me?"

"Not tonight, love. Not tonight."

Chapter 38

"And when your sorrow is comforted
As time soothes all sorrows
You will be content that you have known me.
You will always be my friend.
You will want to laugh with me.
You - you alone will have the stars
as no one else has them...
In one of the stars I shall be living.
In one of them I shall be laughing.
And so it will be as if all the stars were laughing,
When you look at the sky at night...
You - only you –
Will have stars that can laugh."
The Little Prince

The next morning I awaken with a nice-sized bruise on my butt. Man, talk about symbolism. I walk over to the health food store for a green juice and then hit the gym. Returning, I find her in our room folding some of her clothes.

"Pauly, where did you go?"

"It's such a crisp morning I had to get out in it. Here, take a look at this." I lower my pants to show her the blue and purple mark she left.

She makes a strange face. "Did I give you that bruise? Sorry. I didn't mean to. Does it hurt?"

"Not anymore." I sit down on the bed and invite her to do the same.

What do I say and how do I say it?

Things like this are never easy or flawless, so I just speak honestly from the heart.

"Love, I simply cannot do this anymore. I'm done. We have to figure out some of the logistics, but I need for us to separate as soon as possible."

To my surprise, she looks shocked. Did she believe we could or should go on like this? Is my version of insanity her version of normal?

She scans the room and then looks at me. "Can't I stay here and take the next few weeks or months to set up my new life?"

"No. I can't continue to live with you and don't want to repeat all the back and forth from our crazy breakup summer. Besides, I'm not going to have you here while you audition new men, date, and find someone else."

"I could promise you I won't date."

"I hate to be blunt, but right now your promises to me are worthless. Though well-intentioned in the moment, they carry no weight."

"Pauly, you can't quit. You always quit. You have to learn about commitment. You have to stay committed."

"Miracle, I've been thinking about it, and I'm all about commitment. I meditate every day, I go to the gym, I can sit for a year and write, and there are friends I've held closely in my life for over thirty years. I'm committed to God, truth, love, kindness, and life, but I won't take such a noble word and pervert it into something dysfunctional.

I'm not committed to addiction, drama, pain, suffering, pettiness, and disease. I'm sorry, but I cannot let your demons castrate my peace. No, love, it's over, and it's time to move on. This kind of life isn't good for either of us."

She appears to think for a moment. "Is this because I've put on so much weight?"

I'm incredulous. "Are you kidding? It doesn't matter what you look like. All of our external beauty changes and fades. No, it's all about addiction, drinking and dysfunction."

She looks lost. "But I have nowhere to go."

"You have to go home."

"But Pauly, I'll die."

"This is the choice you created."

I watch her think some more. "Will you continue to support me for a while? Can I stay on your health insurance? What about my student loans? I'll need money to live on. I can't just go home broke."

I put my hand on her shoulder. "Yes, of course. I will support you for a while. But you'll need to get a job doing something. In the four years we've been together, you have only managed to work for a couple of months. When we met you didn't have a job. I know it's easy for you to get a man to support you, but it's time to stand on your own two feet."

"That's not fair."

"You realize you've never been alone."

"I hate being alone." She says darkly.

"Well, my pretty friend, something tells me you won't be for long. We both know you're exceptionally good at finding someone."

"Pauly, please don't be mean."

"Come on, it's true."

"You seem so unemotional and cold. I guess you hate me at this point."

"No, of course not. I just feel done. I'm sure it will hit me later in waves and waves. But let's figure this out today and move on."

"Today?"

"Yes. I'm serious about ending it. It's over. Call your parents and make the arrangements. Find a flight for tomorrow, and let's just move on."

She gets up slowly, goes into the bathroom and closes the door.

I get in the car and unconsciously drive over to the lake. After walking in numbness for a period of time, I sit beneath an old hickory tree and cry.

When I return a few hours later, she is spread across our bed. "Pauly, are you sure you no longer want to be together?"

I sit down next to her and gently put my hand on her back. "Yes, love, sadly I am."

"I talked to my parents. They are traveling for a couple of weeks. I guess I can go home and stay with my sister, at least in the short term. Maybe we just need a break again to see things clearly."

I feel her breathing body rising and falling slowly. "Did you check on flights?"

She looks sad, perhaps hoping I would have a sudden change of heart. "Yes, I can leave tomorrow in the morning."

I take an inner inventory and feel dead inside. "Ok then..."

Of course I feel terribly sad about this, but at this point I just want this nightmare to end. I want my life back. I want to live in peace again.

The day drifts by and I do a lot of odds and ends to distract myself from the pain of the moment.

I go back to the health food store to grab some lunch and run into Peter Pan. Always a keen observer, he asks, "Are you doing all right? You look a bit pale."

"She's leaving tomorrow morning for the west coast."

His eyes widen. "It's over?"

"Yes."

He shakes his head. "Man, I'm sorry, but to be honest, I'm also kind of relieved. Of course, I couldn't help but witness what's been going on the past few weeks, hell, the whole year, and I believe you deserve better than this. It is insanity, and there's no reason to accept it. Life is too short."

This candor surprises me, because Peter P is usually reticent, even when prodded, to give his opinion on this sort of personal stuff. "Wow, really?"

He shakes his head with conviction. "Look, I like her and I know she's compelling, and no doubt the sex is other-worldly, but why put up with all the other malarkey? Plus, I talked to her the other day, and she was just out of it."

"It's those crazy pain pills she takes for her headaches."

Peter gazes at the buffet and then at me. "Look, I've been living with both of you for the past few months, and to my eyes you do most of the giving. You make her coffee, do the dishes, the laundry, and most of the cleaning. Hell, you even pay the bills! What's fair about this dynamic?"

"She says she's a 'feeler' and not a 'do-er, but..."

"What? Come on, man, that's cosmic bullshit. She's just spoiled and lazy. It's not all her fault, either."

I look out the window. "The Miracle brings a lot of wonderful intangibles when she's in her true self. It's not all black and white. But she does suffer from the Princess Syndrome."

"I'm sure she's been catered to since she was young because she's so insanely beautiful." Peter says. "Life has bent over backwards for her, but the irony is, in the end that paradigm does more damage than good."

"Why?"

"With all the focus on her looks, her inner game remains overlooked and undeveloped. Instead of reading something substantial, she looks at those silly magazines about celebrities and the latest diets." We hit the checkout line and Peter Pan pulls out some cash. "Here, I'm buying your lunch."

"But..."

"Come on, I got this." He pays the cashier and we take a seat.

He shakes his head. "The pills, the drinking, and all of the crazy bullshit. What does she bring besides her beauty? Again, with time looks are going to fade."

"The Miracle is much more than a pretty face and yes, I know, it's silly for me to defend her. But I've seen her soul and she is..." I can't finish. "I will say this: being with her has made me a better man. There has been a ton of growth, but sadly, not enough on my end to make it all work."

"Your end? Pauly, she has no idea who she is and she's looking to you to fill that vast hole. She is a classic example of the 'discouraged' child and it's only a matter of time before she moves into the 'revenge' phase of her dysfunction, if she hasn't already. She will ultimately end up dropping you for someone new."

"I guess that's possible. The drinking does make her unpredictable."

"Exactly. Better to be grateful you got a vocation out of it, learned a ton, and move on. Thank the stars above you don't have a baby with her. Can you imagine spending the rest of your life trying to deal with this shit as it gets progressively worse?"

This makes me shudder. "You are very perspicacious."

"Look, man, I was there in Del Mar when you met her. It was a classic rescue. She had no place to live, no money, a trail of debts, and her roommate claimed she was a sociopath."

"And we thought the roommate was nuts. Thinking about it now, I can clearly see that all the warning signs were conveniently ignored." My mind drifts back to the beaches of Del Mar and the halcyon days of our coming together. "Peter, do you remember all of us, even the Little Gypsy having lunch that one sunny day at the Cardiff Market?"

He looks out through the window. "I do. Wasn't there a book fair or something going on?"

"Yes. The four of us seemed so happy with our lives joyfully intertwined, and now we come to a point where we will all be inhabiting separate places."

He considers this. "Life is so unpredictable." I can see the deep concern and caring for me in his eyes. "Again, be thankful you came out of this relatively intact. Perhaps a bit wounded, but ultimately more whole."

I wipe my eyes. "You're probably right, but man, it still hurts."

"Of course it does, and it's okay to cry, to feel it. But I knew it was going to end when she started to interfere with your art, with your writing, like she knew anything. I mean, that was a deal breaker. Then there was all the insane spending, and that's never going away."

"Well, at least there will be no more fights." I shake my head and wipe my eyes again.

"And what about her drinking? I mean, you don't even touch alcohol, so there's no alignment. How could this have ever worked out?"

"Man, when you put it like this, there is clarity."

"Brother, I'm sad for you. I mean, it's going to hurt for a while, but in the long run you'll be better off. Again, thank God you don't need a couple of expensive attorneys like so many people do, or have a child with a crazy drunk mommy. You're getting off easy, my friend."

Not many people will respect you enough to tell you the tough truths. I put my hand on his shoulder. "Peter, you're a hell of a friend. What would I have done without you?"

"Hey, it goes both ways." He laughs. "So after she leaves and you start feeling nostalgic, remember to grab the old rusty key you used to give me and go outside in the rain and see if it'll work."

I smile, remembering us at the table. "Ah yes, the ultimate exercise in futility."

He then tosses out, "Trying to rescue another person who refuses to take responsibility for their life, that is the embodiment of futility."

"Classic stuff. I will probably have to use the key a few times, mostly at night before bed."

"That's funny and true." He stands up. "If you do, just think about Christmas and all those over-priced presents for about five minutes. That should help."

I crack up. "Touché. Which reminds me, I need to find the box with the crazy angel ornament and bury it in the back yard."

He raises an eyebrow. "Don't tempt the fates. Hey, you can always come down to Mexico. The sun and surf would probably do you well."

"It's worked in the past." I get up and we share a long hug. "I'll see you back at the hacienda. Thank you."

"You're welcome, my brother."

I send my buddy a text. "The Miracle ends tomorrow. She's going back home. Please instruct the troops to hang all the flags at half-mast."

A moment later, he writes back. "Don't cry because it's over, smile because it happened. --Dr. Seuss. Love you brother."

I call Saint Bonnie and set up an appointment for later in the week. Keeping a space for healing will be essential to get my trajectory back on track.

My phone rings.

"Pauly, can we get a bottle of champagne and just have a happy last night?"

What can I say at this point? We only have about 14 hours left...

"Sure honey, why not..."

"Don't worry about picking it up. I'll take a walk over myself. I need to get out of the house."

Come evening, as usual, it is drinks for one. She offers me a glass.

"Won't you at least have a sip?"

I take the glass but don't partake.

We sit in the bedroom and, for a while, talk about a variety of meaningless things while ignoring the elephant in the room.

Finally I say, "I think we long for what we once had and lost during that exquisite period of time back in Del Mar and our first year in Nashville. Back when we moved as one in harmony. We would meditate, converse and connect. There was no drinking or drama, just love and peace. We miss what we were."

She looks at me winsomely. "We did have some wonderful times."

I manage a sad smile. "We sure did. But we are no longer those people, so we can't go back to a place that no longer exists."

She looks down. "I'm sorry it didn't work out."

"Me too, my love."

She gives me a sly smile. "At least the sex was fabulous."

I chuckle. "The sex was transcendent."

Speaking of sex, when she finishes the bottle she is ready for some action. She disappears into the closet and returns in breathtaking form, wearing titillating black lingerie. "Remember this from the Vineyard?"

How sad...

Her long hair is flowing down across her shoulders, her olive skin still tan from our days on the beaches of the Vineyard. Those voluptuous curves and full breasts, still take my breath away. But now there is something tragic about it all.

Yes, she is erotic. But what about the rest of the stuff?

She comes over to me and gives me a kiss, the taste of champagne on her moist, full lips.

"Pauly, come to bed with me. Make love to me one last time."

"I don't know, love. I'm feeling quite blue about it all."

"Please, Pauly. It's our last night."

~~~

With some encouragement from her, the primal drive of life takes over and we engage in what we do best. I let my passion pour out of me and into her, riding the powerful waves of desire as the candles sparkle around the room. When we reach the summit and our essences merge, time stops its endless march for a moment and we lock eyes as one.

A few seconds later, we both burst into tears, our hearts and emotions pouring forth, two refugees in the wilderness, mourning our magic and madness. Ours was a magnificent dance, with epic highs and lows, yet in the end we are left with a bittersweet taste, a matrix of complex stories and deep scars.

A few hours later, I wake up in the middle of the night to the sound of rain and thunder. She is out cold with assistance of heavy inebriation. Eyes closed, I listen to the raindrops against the window and the sound of her breathing.

What a shame...

The Beatles song 'Long & Winding Road' plays gently in my head.

> The wild and windy night
> That the rain washed away
> Has left a pool of tears
> Crying for the day
> Why leave me standing here
> Let me know the way

I wonder... should I cancel her flight and hang in there? If she gets on that plane, she's probably never coming back. God gave us a second chance, and we couldn't make it. How sad for us, how sad for love. I will be going back to the emptiness of single life. Will I ever find my partner? Where's my true love?

My mind covers a lot of ground as the rain outside intensifies. I try to remember the best of us, but all I can recall is pain.

I get up to use the bathroom and see the empty champagne bottle backlit by a tiny wall light.

Oh the irony of this image, which feels like the symbol of our demise. I once again recall my Aunt Joan and her drunken blind rages, the hopelessness in my Uncle's eyes, and know I could never live that life.

I see lightning through the cracks of the drapes and off in the distance hear a bit of brontide.

Yes, it's over. The period ahead will be tough. What will I do and where will I go?

Meanwhile, in my heart, the Beatles silently play on...

> Many times I've been alone
> And many times I've cried
> Anyway you'll never know
> The many ways I've tried

I open the drapes and allow the soft evening light to illuminate her angelic face.

What a captivating girl, with such inner demons.

Has it been four years since she walked into that kitchen in Del Mar and changed my life forever? How could I ever regret spending time with her? Yes, no love is ever wasted. Sometimes you have to be brave enough to break your own heart.

My whole being throbs with pain and my stomach hurts as a streak of light passes through the room and over us.

God, I so want to hold her and tell her I won't ever let go, that I understand what happened to her and she has finally found refuge here with me. Let her demons rage against us like the storm outside. We can withstand them and anything, because my life without her will not be as vibrant and alive, the colors not as bright, and my world so much colder.

But still they lead me back
To the long and winding road
You left me standing here
A long, long time ago
Don't keep me waiting here
Lead me to your door

I gingerly get back into bed and gently pull her to me. She instinctively melts into my embrace.

It's not over yet. She's here now. Tomorrow this bed will feel cavernous, empty, and cold... just like the inside of me... but in this moment our bodies are naked and warm. I remember the first night we made love and how we slept throughout the night so tightly intertwined.

Two souls finally reunited in form after eons spent wandering the galaxies searching for each other and this embrace. I had never felt such an utter sense of spiritual completion.

Yes, in a few short hours, the void awaits me. The void always awaits us, yet through grace we are sometimes given a brief and fleeting clemency.

276

The light of the dawn appears to be awakening. A new day and the opportunity for infinite possibilities awaits.

Should I cancel the flight? There's still time.

Simone Weil said, "There are only two things that pierce the human heart: beauty and affliction; moments we wish would last forever, and moments we wish had never begun. What are we to make of these messengers?"

I get up and my whole body hurts, perhaps a culmination of all of it. My ass still has a nice bruise on it and for some reason I find this funny.

She wakes up with a huge hangover and sour disposition, the polar opposite of the woman who fell asleep in my arms. Perhaps this is life's way of making our parting easier?

We ride to the airport silently. As we pull into the terminal, she says, "I'll call you tonight to let you know I got there safely."

"Yes, love, please do. Are you feeling any better?"

"No. My whole body hurts. I took a pill, so I'll sleep on the plane."

More silence...

I pull up to the curb. This is it. Ironically, for all the buildup, the moment is actually quite simple and practical. Two giant bags are taken from the trunk of the car and handed to a skycap.

"Pauly, do you have any cash?"

I reach into my pocket and give her all I have. There is one long, last hug. "I love you, Pauly."

"I love you too, Miracle."

"Pauly… please don't forget me."

I squeeze her tighter. "Never. Never, my love."

She buries her face into my chest. "Thank you so much for everything."

"I love you, dear one…"

"I love you too, sweet Pauly."

As we finally let go, I see tears coming down her cheeks from behind the dark glasses.

Perhaps, in the end, we were just two comets that intersected briefly together there in the dark and endless sky.

Perhaps, in the end, we are all like that.

We hug again, kiss on the lips, and then release.

She turns from me, gathers herself for a moment and departs. She never looks back. I watch her pass through the sliding glass doors and out of sight.

For a few moments I stand there looking at those doors, wondering if she might walk back out and refuse to leave.

What a ride, what a story, and what a love. Thank you, Miracle.

I shake my head as the sun breaks briefly through the clouds and casts a warm ray of light upon my face. For a split second the chill in me ceases, but only for an instant.

In the end, her arrival and departure are as mysterious to me as all things.

I get back in the car but just sit there silently. A deep breath and a long exhale. Then another…

A policeman with a kind face taps gently on my window.

"Sir, it's time to move on."

I somehow manage a smile.

"Yes, it is."

From Book 3

"7 Crazy Days In Maui"

The Call

*"The hero's journey always begins with the call.
There is a whole aspect of your consciousness, your being,
that's not been touched."*
Joseph Campbell

As the brilliant, Maui sunshine cascades down upon me, unimpeded by a single cloud, I sit on the golden sand and watch a pair of mighty humpback whales breech off the South coast.

My phone vibrates with a number I don't recognize.

"Hello?... Hello?"

"Pauly?"

"Yes..."

"I.. I want... I wondered..." I hear the sound of crying and then... "I cannot go on another day like this. I simply do not want to live anymore. I don't... I do not have the energy to keep faking it while surrounded by people who so deeply hate me."

The voice on the other end of the line is raw, the sobs become heavy and heartfelt. The despair is palatable, and her breathing shallow, as she tries in vain to regain her frail composure.

"Miracle... Miracle, is that you?"

Silence. "Please, give me... I need a moment... to..."

"Sure." The waves in the water come in sets that appear to be in sync with her sobs.

"Pauley, you are the only one who has ever really loved me, seen me, and supported me. I have to find a way to come back to you. I need to see you again, if only to be around your bright Light and positive vibrations.

Long pause...

"Will you let me come home? I need to come home. Please let me come home."

She softly weeps as I listen silently. Her primal cries pierce the marble walls I have so meticulously constructed to protect me. Time, distance, neglect, disrespect, insensitivity, and deceit have changed none of the powerful feelings connected to this one woman.

My mind drifts back over our barren landscape of wasted years in self-imposed mutual exile. Like a butterfly randomly dancing between flowers, my memory pauses briefly on moments from our past: warm embraces, tender smiles, pettiness, afflictions, addictions, and erotic interludes.

Has she finally hit the bottom? Finally? But it feels much too late. That part of me that loved her so deeply has died a long time ago, not all at once, but from a thousand different cuts.

I am pulled back from my daydream to the present by her gentle whisper, "Are you there?"

"Yes, I'm sorry."

"Pauley, can I please come home?"

Acknowledgements

Thank you...

Thank you...

To all the amazing people who read my first book, *Hitchhiking With Larry David*, and let me know how much my words meant to you through countless notes, hugs, encounters, stories and moments shared in presence. Your love and support empowered me to write the book you are holding in your hands.

I hope you will stay in touch.

To my oldest friends who also happen to be my amazing parents, I love you deeply.

Your life of sacrifice and service enabled me to embody a life of opportunity with all infinite possibilities. You taught me that with enough hard work, any dream was within my grasp. Lastly, your sixty-eight year love affair is a monument to caring and commitment. I feel blessed to not only be a witness to your life story, but a living example of it.

Saint Katherine of Lott... my spiritual sister in laughter, learning, love and mischief... Thank you for stepping up and out... thus filling the world with so much light... Everything you touch improves and glows...

To a large group of Angels cleverly disguised as my beautiful friends. It has been such a privilege to be a part of your lives.

In no particular order...

To the Great Simmons and his lovely family, who generously offer me their home and hearts on my never frequent enough visits to Nashville. David, I appreciate your support and guidance, all your creative suggestions-especially on my books, and how you always expect more from me... while loving me just as I am.

To the one and only Peter Pan who helped me enormously on Hitchhiking With Larry David and continues to be a wonderful portal of wisdom, observation and humor. I am so happy that Love Found You.

Annabelle Jackman who was gracious enough to read this book and offer some wonderful insights. You are such a sweet soul and I appreciate you always seeing for me the BIG picture. Good dog!

Karen B. my pint sized spirit sister who overflows with love, enthusiasm and awareness and then showers it all over the people blessed enough to be around her.

My Brother Billy Block who comes to me with his warm sunshine smile and easy laugh. Even though you are always here... I miss seeing you.

Brother Malcolm for the endless hours we share and grow together. Ma Bevins...! Montanez Wade & Brenda Gilbert~ Norm the Giver... Kevin & Tahra, Tom Marvel, George Green, Merilynn & Romantic Mike, Tracy & Drew, Raquel & Geoff, Mosto-piece, John Dowd Jr, Ron Cook.

To one of my MV Patron Saints Dudley...

Vineyard Family: Ann & Mark Ide, Rita and Frank on Circuit, Terrell & Kim, Priscilla and Ned, Water Street

Wendy also known as Cindy, Tony on 19th Street, Rabbi Jim, Pat and April, Vasska and Tarni, Suzanne, Colin, Scarlet Keyes, Luke Store-walker, The Brandt Clan, Angela Hahn and the girls... and the loving memory of my dear friend Andrew Brandt.

The wonderful people at the Edgartown Bookstore!

Lynn, Chris and Jack... May you always be filled with Grace.

Alan Brewer, another generous patron and long time friend of mine who gave me a home base in the city of angels as well as a robust friendship.

David Sanford-my brother from another mother...

The Fabulous Desage Family and Queen D who rules her kingdom with kindness, humor and grace; Debra you are one of the most generous people I have ever met and I will always treasure our Beverly Hills adventures together.   Beam me up!

Shauna M, Jill Mclure and her clan, Neil Warren, Robert Matsuda...

Nashville: Lucas P. Gravel, Saint Dennis Martin, Dan Maddox, Mike Bodayle, Kevin/Clyde, Melissa Meadows...

My Beloved Bonnie Johnson... for the endless hours of love, support, and healing!

Angel Barb & Izzy in Maui... you embody the Aloha... You too Autumn Shields! Alexia, Tiffany Love, and Chris & Sara at the scooter shop...

My wise and loving Agent Angela, for all her time and effort

Matthew Wayne Selznick, who did a fantastic job editing the book and in the process turned me into a much better writer. Then, as icing on the cake, became a good friend.

To my Brother Chris who I will always love with all of my heart.

And To The Miracle... you saw in me beautiful words and unlimited potential, and invited to me to live from a higher place and to share my gifts. Though in the end our dance was far too short and ultimately ended in sorrow, you made me a better man.

Thank you~

Please stay in touch!

Send me your Miracle stories & pictures with the book!

Email:

mvyhitchhiker@gmail.com

Facebook:

http://www.facebook.com/home.php?#!/profile.php?id=731140460

https://www.facebook.com/mvymiracles?skip_nax_wizard=true&ref_type=bookmark

Twitter:

@psdhitchhiker

Please visit my site:

www.paulsamueldolman.com

CPSIA information can be obtained
at www.ICGtesting.com
Printed in the USA
BVOW04s2306040917
493950BV00003B/34/P